PERFECT 10

Writing and Producing the Ten-Minute Play

Gary Garrison

HEINEMANN
PORTSMOUTH, NH

Heinemann
A division of Reed Elsevier Inc.
361 Hanover Street
Portsmouth, NH 03801–3912
www.heinemanndrama.com

Offices and agents throughout the world

Library of Congress Cataloging-in-Publication Data
Garrison, Gary.
Perfect 10 : writing and producing the ten-minute play / Gary Garrison.
p. cm.
ISBN 0-325-00312-2 (pbk. : alk. paper)
1. Drama—Technique. 2. Playwriting. 3. Theater—Production and direction.
4. One-act plays—History and criticism. 5. One-act plays, American.
I. Title: Writing and producing the ten-minute play. II. Title: Perfect ten.
III. Title: Writing and producing the 10-minute play. IV. Title.

PN1661 .G36 2001
808.2'41—dc 21

00-069702

Editor: Lisa A. Barnett
Production: Vicki Kasabian
Cover design: Jenny Jensen Greenleaf
Author photo: Dave Cross Photography
Manufacturing: Steve Bernier

Printed in the United States of America on acid-free paper
05 04 03 02 01 VP 1 2 3 4 5

To my mom and dad,
'cause something should always be dedicated to those
who've helped you through this life with love . . .

CONTENTS

Contents

ACKNOWLEDGMENTS

FIRST AND FOREMOST, A SPECIAL THANKS GOES TO MY EDITOR AT Heinemann, Lisa Barnett, for liking my first book enough to publish a second, and for believing that something as short as a ten-minute play deserves a whole book.

To Jason T. Garrett, my over-the-shoulder editor: never stray far. I need your brilliance, generosity, and sassy wit always close by. Alright, mistuh!

To Cathy Norgren, Gregg Henry, and Jay Edelnant for allowing me to take to the wind and fly with it everywhere I went, and to Mary Monroe, who so often was right beside me with her guidance and patience. BDG adores you all like no other.

To my colleague, coproducer, and close friend, Maggie Lally, for suffering through producing one ten-minute play festival after another at NYU with me, and for never losing her sense of humor when I lost mine for the gazillionth time.

To my mentor and friend, Mark Dickerman, for the example he sets at NYU for all teachers and dramatists. Thanks for the free time when I announced, "I have to write."

To Michel Wallerstein, Wendy Yondorf, Gary Sunshine, Tish Benson, and David Crespy for sharing your talent and your artistry in this book. Bravo. You inspire me.

Finally, to all the playwrights that I've spoken to in a public forum about your work: I often had more to say about your play, but unfortunately not enough time to say it. So I said what I thought you needed to hear. I know that a writer can never hear enough about his work, so what was left to say, I've said in this book. It's because of you that I wrote it. Thanks, from the bottom of my heart, for the inspiration.

INTRODUCTION

I'M SPINNING THIS BIG OL' FANTASY IN MY HEAD AND AS EACH steamy, smoggy, try-to-catch-your-breath New York day passes, it gets more whacked, more tightly woven into my dramatic imagination: somewhere in the cosmos, Lillian Hellman is lounging in a big, red, over-stuffed easy chair (Pottery Barn, fall collection), legs clamped at the ankles, smoking, drinking, and chattin' up the boys—Aristotle, Shakespeare, Ibsen, O'Neill, and Williams. No one's in a good mood. Lillian's tanked and shouting only the choicest four-letter words to the heavens; Tennessee's tanked and cursing his last ten years in the theatre; Eugene's depressed—again; Henrik's in a perpetual state of wondering what language people are speaking; Bill's pissing everybody off by writing quietly in a corner; and Tots (Lillian's name for Aristotle) is curiously humming "The Battle Hymn of the Republic."

Lillian tosses one back, slams the shot glass down on the table and barks/slurs, "Well, what the hell should we expect? For God's sake, the whole culture's been racing the clock since someone screamed, 'When's the damn turkey gonna be ready?' at Plymouth Rock! If it isn't fast, it isn't American. They go to school quick, get a job quick, make money quick, attract a mate quick, build the nest quick, vacation in Maui quick, and then finally race for a place to lay the coffin! They produce fewer children, eat less food, read less, sleep less, and keep less. So, of course, they're gonna *write* less 'cause people wanna *watch* less. Thou canst like it or lump it, Billy Boy, but the ten-minute play is here to stay!"

O'Neill gasps, blurts out something about the tyranny of women, and buries his head in his arms; Ibsen screams for an immediate translation; Williams wonders if Hellman's fab dress comes in a size 16; Shakespeare dots the *i* in *finis* and deadlifts his six-hundred-page manuscript to a coffee table; and Aristotle offers simply: "Se parakalo, pirasi mou to kre-as me tis elli-es" (loose Greek translation: *Please pass the olive loaf*).

Back to reality. I wonder, if they're not concerned, then why am I?

Because you and I are witness to an honest-to-god, baby-it's-real, don't-look-now brand-new genre of theatre that's feverishly pushing its way into the sunshine. Others want to disregard it as a trifling weed, but I dare you to try to pull it from the dirt, 'cause it won't happen. Can't happen. It's too strong. Too late. Too dug in. So I've got this nagging feeling that we'd better all understand what's growing in our own backyards.

I wouldn't be crazy enough to label this a "how to write a ten-minute play" book, but I will suggest that what follows is a brief (I mean, we are talking about ten minutes as the focus here, cowboys and cowgirls) guide for writing the newest form. If you're a playwright, consider this a primer for what makes good, compelling theatre and discover how that has no less a place in these little hors d'oeuvre dramas. If you're a theatre manager, a director, or an artistic director, we're going to look at the very real practicalities of producing ten-minute plays. We'll also examine five different writers' approaches to the same thematic idea in constructing a ten-minute play and discover how singularity of voice is every bit as true in a tightly constricted form. And last, you're going to write your own ten-minute play and explore it, dramaturgically, through the ideas presented in the book.

A word of caution: Like all creative ventures, the process takes longer than the product. And that's a good thing. Don't take the title of the book wrong: I'm not trying to get you to write a perfect ten-minute play; I'm trying to perfect *you* writing a ten-minute play.

$$1$$

CHAPTER

Bones for the Pickin'

I appreciate the form most when it's really the only option that could possibly contain the experience the writer wishes to give the audience. I don't like it when I feel short-shrifted, when I'm left hungry for more. Or when the writer uses the form to tell a quick joke. I'd rather hear a quick joke over a Whopper Junior. —Gary Sunshine, playwright

OH . . . MY . . . GOD. WE'VE CREATED A MONSTER, AND WE DON'T even know it.

In the time it takes to sort through a pile of almost-white cotton socks from your dryer, whip up three eggs over-easy, or watch Celine Dion come in or out of retirement, you could witness the newest double-edged sword the American theatre has to offer: the ten-minute play. Look in any small- to medium-size theatre or educational institution across the country, and you're bound to smack right up against it. And it seems the trend is growing faster than anyone can keep up with.

Has it ever happened before that a generation of artists have embraced a new creative form with such wild energy and enthusiasm, completing whole, dramatic creations in the time it takes to languorously eat a slice of pepperoni pizza? I never even saw it coming. Did you? And where the heck did it come from? I wagered a guess in an article I wrote for *The Dramatists Guild Newsletter* in January 1999:

First there was the full-length play about a ga-jillion years ago. Then some sassy, know-it-all playwright got daring (or maybe bored, or low on ink, or was a victim of attention deficit disorder) and thought, "why do in three long, *long* acts what you can do in one?" So the one-act play became the genre du jour until God created television and MTV. Then some clever playwright thought, "why do in one act what you can do in ten minutes or in a monologue play?" Shortly thereafter, God created Jane Martin and/or the Actors Theatre of Louisville, and the great submission flood rivaled its biblical equivalent. But sadly, pretty much every playwright's ten-minute play just died in the flood.

So God created the *Dramatists Sourcebook* and *The Playwright's Companion*, and lo and behold, there appeared the One-Page Play. Wonder if God's going to create an audience for it? (If so, expect the next Great Flood.) Pretty soon we'll have the No Page Play—and just a lot of playwrights lined up at the door of a literary manager who sits patiently listening to a writer say, "Just imagine a play . . . and it's really funny . . ."

. . . I shouldn't be surprised; none of us should: we are a generation of writers raised on television. We know the world in sound-bites and out-takes. Our television programming, commercials, and films are doled out in fifteen- to thirty-second images that flash only the condensation of emotion, with little screen time spent watching those emotions develop. We are used to an abbreviated expression of creativity. And I, as a teacher of playwriting, have to constantly work against that conditioning in the classroom, and then wrestle with it myself in my own creative soul . . .

Don't get me wrong, I like the ten-minute play. I'm a real sucker for it. I should be—every one I've written has been produced. But it wasn't enough that they be *my* creative best friend: I wanted *everybody* to love them. So I started a Ten-Minute Play Festival at NYU for the Dramatic Writing Program, another for my region of the Kennedy Center's American College Theatre Festival (which has now evolved into a national ten-minute play festival), another for Off-Off Broadway's Pulse Ensemble Theatre, another for the Playwrights Program of the Association for Theatre in Higher Education, and a few others that I've forgotten because the experience was . . . well, brief. I've championed the ten-minute play to my writer friends and students for the last five years as a new, exciting variation for the theatre—a writer's challenge, a great exercise for actors, a director's dream, a producer's profitable night at the box office.

That is until one day, about a year ago, when I was sitting—where else?—in an Off-Off Broadway theatre watching an evening of ten-minute plays that were really *bad*, really *long*, and had about as much appeal as watching Henry Kissinger read from a telephone book. I recalled a healthy number of the four or five hundred ten-minute plays I'd read, thought of all of those I had produced (about half that many), and gulped—a big, lugubrious gulp that most of the Third World must have heard and that's still lodged in my throat. Why?

Because very few writers know what they're creating when they write them, what to do with them once they're written, or what to do with the skills they learned while writing the short play when and if they finally sit down to write a long one. At the core of all of this is a very simple prob-lem: few playwrights have thought about what these plays really are or what they should try to be and what magic or disaster they can create for their audience. Writers seem to universally acknowledge one thing: they're short, and it feels easier, because "how many mistakes can you make in such a short amount of time?"

A lot. A load. Tons of them. So many you'd think you've never written a single word in your life. Shorter doesn't mean easier on any level. Ahhh, there's the rub. Filling the empty space with evocative language, fascinat-ing characters, and a compelling story all in ten minutes is harder to do than any of us thinks, but we haven't spent much time thinking about it because it's all so new. Look, I know they're great fun to write, they're good learning tools for any writer, they're terrific acting and directing exercises, and they're a fabulous way of introducing a large number of writers to an audience in one pop. But there are very real, very solvable problems in the creation of this form that, if we just stop in our zealous-ness to create, we can solve with some good, sound dramaturgical thought in such a way that everyone wins. Before any of that can happen, however, I have to try to tackle my dread about the whole of it and pick a few bones with myself and the rest of the theatre world before encourag-ing anyone to write a ten-minute play.

BONE NO. 1: RIGHT OR WRONG, SHORT FOR LONG

Call me reactionary, but I get scared when I see my art form shrinking with such wild abandonment. I'm concerned that we're encouraging a new genre for a generation of writers not necessarily proficient or prolific in the long forms. I'm hesitant (but do it anyway) to teach my students how to write ten-minute plays when I know they haven't fully embraced the one-act play, let alone the full-length play. When I teach them the ten-minute play form, am I only reinforcing what ails them in the first place? And for myself, I'm afraid if I keep writing them I might lose or dull the fragile skills it's taken me years to learn writing the longer forms. The American theatre needs writers who can write full-length plays! Look on Broadway! We're not there! The Brits are there. And sometimes the Irish when they can elbow their way past the Brits. Everybody's pounding American dramatists into obscurity—and we're all letting them.

And yet writing a ten-minute play is just so tempting because the whole thing is, well, it's so friggin' short. In one afternoon, I can write a ten-minute play, do a thirty-pound load of wash, do a rewrite, water the dead plants, do another rewrite, paint my bathroom, and be back at the computer to do a polish before I hear Tom Brokaw gargle, "Good evening." And believe it or not, that scares me, if not for myself then for other writers, because it *feels* easy. But if you've written long enough, you know nothing about it is easy and nothing about it is quick.

I can be at peace with this emerging form only if I make a commitment to use the same skills and creative know-how in writing the short form as with the long. And maybe that's where all of this goes awry. I mean, shouldn't the ten-minute play be some style of story-driving dramatic action that has some sort of resolution and that lasts for ten minutes? It shouldn't be what amounts to just a scene or a Saturday Night Live sketch; it's probably not a monologue; and it's definitely not a dance/poetry reading/choral ode to the universe's biosystem, but unfortunately, that's what I'm experiencing in the theatre when I see them time and again.

BONE NO. 2: SHORT MEANS THIN

As I've traveled about the country, either for the Kennedy Center or by way of my own career as a writer and teacher, the number of bad ten-minute plays I've seen in the last three years has been enough to rock the dead. I couldn't even say, "Thank God they were only ten minutes," because the truth of the matter is few writers clock in on time. Recently I had the good fortune of traveling to eight different regions of the country as a member of the National Selection Team for the Kennedy Center's American College Theatre Festival. Each region presented a ten-minute play festival, producing the work of college playwrights from the area. To my mind, I could find myself in no better circumstance that would illuminate the "state of the union" of this relatively new genre. Of the eighty or so ten-minute plays I saw or read, here's what I experienced, first by topic:

I'm a boy, you're a girl, what's-the-difference-between-us?-Oh-it's-just-understanding-and/or-consensually-embracing-our-different-equipment kind of play. (11)

I'm gay, you're gay, he's gay, she's gay, my roommate/father/mother/uncle/rabbi/doctor/dentist/lawyer/teacher/mailman/pastor/accountant/massage therapist and-the-President-of-the-United-States-is-probably-gay kind of play. (18)

The "fuck" plays (their word, not mine): "I fucked you when he wasn't looking, but you fucked him when you were looking right at me. So that's it. No more fucking . . . unless you want to. Truth is, I hate sex but what else can we do on a Friday night?" (12)

Saturday Night Live sketches-as-plays: What would happen if the world was suddenly overtaken by sponges? Who's more important, Mr. Cheese or Mr. Cracker? Armpits have feelings, too. (15)

The "jump" plays: jumping centuries, jumping planets, jumping solar systems, jumping gender, jumping rope (believe it or not, not as bad you'd think), jumping realities/plains/levels/dimensions/personalities/diseases. (8)

The terrorist plays: Anybody who was not Caucasian showed up in these plays with a chip on one shoulder and an uzi on the other. (7)

The poetry plays; three were in iambic pentameter. (4)

The real thing: solid stories with conflict, character, sharp dialogue, and a variety of structures in storytelling that were sometimes conventional, sometimes not. (6)

Of these eighty plays, here's what I experienced in actual time: a third were much longer than ten minutes, a third were longer than ten minutes, and a third earned their classification. Bothersome? You bet. A ten-minute play should be ten minutes, or let's just call it a short play. And as for the sex-fest that dominated the subject matter of these plays, couldn't one make the argument that what I saw was highly appropriate to the age of the writers? Maybe, but good writing is good no matter the age or hormone surge. My issue with these plays was never the subject matter (though I often found it curious), but the thin, almost transparent and superficial treatment of issues of intimacy, gender identity, gender politics, sexuality, nonconsensual sex, AIDS, racism, misogyny, cultural identity, and so on. It takes extraordinary skill to write and develop a full-length play on any of these subjects. So you'd have to be a damn good writer, nay, a *phenomenal* writer to do justice to any of these subjects in a play that lasts only ten minutes.

BONE NO. 3: A WRITER'S ARROGANCE

With a new genre that is constrained by an actual time factor (or page limit) comes the challenge of convincing playwrights to learn the *art* or true skill of writing within its limitations and to recognize that somebody down the line has to actually produce what's been written. A writer's arrogance will make him think that rules or restrictions never quite apply to his art, his masterpiece. And while I'm loathe to put any kind of standard, rule, or aesthetic on a ten-minute play—what true writer would listen anyway?—there has to be some kind of substantive discussion, or refocus, on the genesis of good, involving drama for the sake of audience entertainment no matter what its actual length of performance time. In other words, the real challenge here is to convince writers that the limitations in writing a ten-minute play should be a reason to become *more* creative, not less.

Wheewwww! Okay, I feel better. I just had to give a little voice to those reservations so that we can all start at square one together. Let's keep this in perspective: we're writing ten-minute plays, not discovering the origins of black holes. So if I screw my dramatist's head on right, the ten-minute play should be a self-contained story with compelling characters that advances a conflict and pushes the dramatic tension toward some sort of resolution and (gulp, I hate to use this word) catharsis, no? Isn't that what we expect of most of our theatre experiences? But does that necessarily mean it has to be naturalism or kitchen realism? It doesn't mean that in the long form, so why would it have to be so in the short? After all, Beckett was writing ten-minute plays before we had a new label for them. But what the new form does suggest is that there is little to no time to engage our audience with a dramatically compelling situation, so we have to fight the temptation to be clever or cute, and write idea plays that are thin on the "idea."

We'd all be wise to think this relatively new play-toy through because the truth of the matter is that the ten-minute play isn't going to go away, slipping into obscurity like verse drama, because it has fallen out of fashion. As I write and as you read, it's digging in, pushing its paws into the dirt, wagging its tail in the face of purists, and unwilling to budge because (1) writers perceive it's easy to write, (2) writers get a sense of completion and immediate gratification in a relatively short amount of time, (3) theatres, looking for forums to explore and expose a variety of new voices, are producing record numbers of festivals of new ten-minute plays, (4) they're easy to produce, even by the poorest theatres, and (5) audiences, our livelihood, are beginning to seriously appreciate ten-minute plays and look for their inclusion in a theatre season.

So now that we've thrashed about the good, the bad, and the ugly of it all, let's figure out how to write something that'll make yo' mama shout "Howdy!"

2
CHAPTER

Work Those Ruby Slippers, Dorothy

Since I read hundreds a year, I'm very aware when the writer fulfills the potential of the story . . . —Michael Bigelow Dixon, Literary Manager, Actors Theatre of Louisville

NOBODY LIKES TO BE TOLD WHAT TO DO, ESPECIALLY ME. I'M A Taurus and I defy you to find someone more stubborn, opinionated, and determined than me. While growing up in the South, I was known as bull-headed; when being educated in the North, I became known as a "pain in the ass in class." Why? Because I've never wanted to think in the box. I've always wanted to explore well beyond the box. To insist I go right just about guarantees I'll take a sharp left; demand I paint the sky blue and you'll see cherry red glowing from the heavens; try to convince me there's only one conceivable way to solve a problem and I'll work hard to give you ten solutions. If Glenda the Good Witch had said to me, "Follow the yellow brick road," I would have jumped in with, "What's up with the muddy stone path?" It's not that I intentionally want to be difficult, but I've found that the unexpected, the less obvious or typical, is far more interesting to me as a person and a writer.

Thumbing my nose at rules and regulations has pushed me down some very interesting, exciting, but often troublesome paths; no more so than when I started to learn the craft of playwriting, 'cause there are plenty-o-rules to be broken there. But early on, after I spun in circles for about five years (not attractive at any age), breaking every rule I could find and *getting nowhere*, I realized that I had a choice to make: learn and live by the rules or risk not finding an audience for what I wanted to say. I opted for the former because it was more important for me to find an audience than it was to placate the rebellious little boy in me. And to be really honest with you, part of that conversion was finally admitting to myself that I wasn't clever enough, or maybe even good enough, to defy convention and create my own aesthetic.

You do what you want to do, write what you want to write, 'cause I don't think anyone could convince you otherwise. Stand your ground! Be the writer you want to be. But if that stack of rejection letters gets larger than your desire to sit down and write another play, you might want to rethink your position. You can be the best quarterback in the world, but if you don't have a football team to play on, who's going to know?

But if you are an advice-seeker looking for some direction for writing your ten-minute play that may, in some part, increase its chances for success (however you define that), here are some tools to help you do that. Tools are a means to a very particular end, so you gotta work those ruby slippers, Dorothy, if you wanna get home.

1. CREATE COMPELLING CHARACTERS IN CONFLICT

You will never find a story, plot, theatrical device, notion, idea, or means of expression more interesting than the people, or characters, you create for your play. How could you, really? We're complex, passionate beings who are in a constant state of emotional highs and lows that demand action and reaction. And we're creatures of extremes: not only can we love a person for being what we want, we can also kill her for the same thing. We're fascinating beings that need to be understood through thoughts, reasoning, discussions, rationalizations, memories, and negotiations, to name a very few.

A character created for the stage should reflect at least some small portion of our complexity as human beings. Part of that complexity comes from what he or she wants, needs, desires, and an excellent way to begin the development of any character is to identify those needs in the situation you create for him or her. When we truly want something, it implies an action will follow, and plays, no matter what their length, are all about dramatic action. You're reading this book because your teacher is requiring you to and you *want* a good grade. Or you're reading this book because you *desire* to write a better ten-minute play, because you *need* to be recognized as a good writer, because you *want/desire/need* to derail your friends' and family's doubts that you have what it takes to be a successful writer. In short, you're reading this book because you want something, even if it's just to be mildly distracted for a while. You need, and therefore you take action; it's that simple.

The characters in your play should strongly desire something either from the situation they're in or from one another. It's dramatically strong if they want it, but even stronger if they really need it and must have it for their happiness or well-being: a young college man needs to finally free himself of the memories of childhood abuse when his mother pays him an unexpected visit; morbidly afraid of being alone, an untrusting, older woman needs to find new companionship after the death of her husband; a respected bible school teacher desperately needs to defend his reputation after being accused of sexual harassment. Put these three people/characters on stage in any environment or situation, and you already have the genesis of drama because they will either get what they want or not, and that in and of itself creates a dramatic tension that audiences will watch to see resolved.

The previous examples are situational conflicts—because of a situation he or she finds him- or herself in, the character is forced into taking some sort of action. We can see that every day on television between the hours of 11:00 A.M. and 3:00 P.M.: daytime TV's soap operas. In theatre, we want something deeper, more ponderous, and we get that by extending the situational conflict (Will he or she get what he or she needs?) out to an even larger question: Can we ever really forget or escape our past? How far are we willing to go to not be alone? How tall are the walls we're building around today's teachers? Too tall?

These are pretty hefty questions that don't require a particular style, form, or kind of theatre. They can be posed in a searing drama or an outrageous comedy, but when it's all said and done, and the lights are coming down on your play, you've left your audience with something more than "Will Herbert find true happiness with Lance or will he just leave the godforsaken island once and for all?" Who cares about Herbert and Lance if they're not three-dimensional people that we can identify with? (And with names like Herbert and Lance, they'll need all the attention we can shower on them!) We identify with characters by recognizing in them the same needs, questions, and desires we have.

If you create a central character with a recognizable need or want that pushes him or her to take some sort of action, your next task is really easy: give *everybody* in the play something he or she wants or needs and will either get or not get by the play's end. If you do that, step back and watch the fireworks begin. If I write a play about an overly conscientious, uptight teacher who holds four students after school for detention, and I make that teacher someone that above all else needs to be respected, and I create two students who need to be the center of attention, one student who needs to challenge authority, and one student who needs peace and quiet, the conditions for conflict are great. If I create a fifth character, a principal who needs to pompously exercise her power and authority, who drops in on the class to "observe" the teacher, the conflict—at least for the teacher—increases in a big way when the students misbehave.

You can see, then, how conflict is born just by giving characters very simple things that they want in relation to the other characters. Wouldn't it be more interesting to write the pizza delivery boy as someone who desperately wants to be liked by everyone instead of just the guy who hands over the double-cheese special? Even if he has two lines, he'll be infinitely more interesting. And if in addition to giving him a want or need, you give him some interesting *behaviors*, well, partners, you'll be cooking with gas!

People behave. That's what they do. You can be at a distance, not even know what someone's saying, and still understand some part of the conversation by watching his behavior. I was at the gym today, headphones on tight, listening to some thump, thump, thump music and watching the two people in front of me talk (go figure) as they were running at breakneck speed on their treadmills. Even though their bodies were doing the same mechanical thing, trust me, their emotional bodies and faces were not. One guy clearly thought he was running the New York Marathon, sprinting like he was running through the same field of clover that Julie Andrews sang "Climb Every Mountain" in. You could tell the other poor guy wanted to be that enthusiastic but just couldn't because, clearly, *he hates the gym* and his running shorts kept attacking him. I never heard a word these two guys said, but believe me, I knew a lot about them because I watched them behave.

As a playwright, how can you write characters for the theatre without attaching some sort of behavior to them, behavior that indicates character? As you're reading this you're probably playing with your hair, wiggling your knee, shaking your foot, petting your cat, watching that cute thing walk across the library atrium for the fifth time, eating french fries, or sawing off a fingernail with a sharp bicuspid. But you are doing something. You're physically and emotionally multitasking as you're reading this book.

So why create a character that is only, quite literally, a mouthpiece for saying what you want to say? Wouldn't it be more interesting to write a librarian that wraps rubber bands around her thumbs all morning, then unwraps them all afternoon, as she flirts with the guy who shelves the books? A proud, homeboy from da Bronx is a much more interesting person if he not only wants a date with the young woman on the stoop but spits on her when he talks, habitually trips up the stoop, and always sings a lot—off-key. He wants what he wants—the attention of the young woman—but his behavior is working against him in every conceivable way. A cop is just a cop until he sings Broadway show tunes.

You're asking, "All of this in a ten-minute play?" To which I answer, "Yeah, baby, and it's worse than you think." Within the construction of a ten-minute play, a good deal of this character development has to happen within the first two pages or sooner. We have to know exactly what's at stake for the central character, that is, what she wants/needs/desires and how she behaves, not only in life, but in this particular situation, and we have to establish it *quickly*, because we want to initiate the obstacles that are going to get in her way and produce an emotional struggle for her as she tries get what she wants. We do this much sooner than later in our ten-minute plays because we want to engage our audience fast, unfold the story to keep their attention, and come to some earned resolution that seems plausible and satisfying. It's hard, no doubt about it, but when it works . . . ahhh, it's magic, isn't it?

2. USE A STRUCTURE

I don't have a preference for traditional or nontraditional structures in any play form. But this I do know: there has to be some form of structure that serves the storytelling of the play in an intelligent, thought-provoking way and compels the audience to continue watching your story. One of your challenges as a playwright is to figure out how to best tell your story, either through the traditional structure of a clearly defined beginning, middle, and end, or a variation on that—end, beginning, middle, and then back to end, or just middle and end, or even a more filmlike approach of snippets of conversation that jump time, place, worlds, whatever. But you should make a decision of what will best serve the idea of your play and write from the beginning with that in mind. Clear storytelling, with a structure that supports it, is as important as any character you'll create.

If you write nonlinear, nontraditional structures, you know there's no sense for us to talk about what happens on page one, three, or eight since you uniquely define it by its very creation. Let me warn you, though, that even for just ten minutes, an audience needs to have an emotional attachment to something—person, place, or thing—and it's hard to get emotionally engaged in an intellectual, emotional, or philosophical idea when the stimulus that's presented is too random or obtuse.

If you're someone who's most comfortable with the traditional three-part structure that has a clear beginning, middle, and end, I suggest that the conflict of the play, or the central dramatic question that will be answered during the course of the play (in *The Glass Menagerie*: Will Tom escape the painful memories of his past? In *Amadeus*: Did Salieri murder Mozart? In *A Doll's House*: will Torvald discover Nora's secret?), be positioned somewhere around the first line of the play.

What?!

That's right. I'm suggesting that you start the play closer to its middle and *imply* the beginning of the story throughout the scenes that follow. In other words, let's get right to the action. Start the play with the circumstances already heightened. Let's throw the audience right square-dab into the spin cycle. Think about this way: Let's say you were going to start a play with the scenario of a couple arguing about their relationship. He's not happy, she not's happy, she thinks he's cheating on her because he's grown cold, even aloof. He doesn't kiss her anymore, he never touches her, and he hasn't said a romantic thing to her in years. She might even say something like, "If I didn't know better, I'd say you were trying to push me away, get rid of me." Outraged, he leaves the apartment, slamming the door.

She crosses to the couch, furious, picks up the remote, and surfs the televison channels. The doorbell rings. She turns off the TV, closes her robe with a tight twist of the belt, crosses to a mirror, checks her hair, crosses to the door, looks through the peep hole, and says, "Who is it?" She hears somebody mumble something, decides it's safe and opens the door, then steps back and gasps. You could do that—with at least two pages' worth of your script, minimum—but do we really need to see all of that stuff?

Why not this: Lights up, the door's already open, the woman in the robe takes a step back and gasps, and in walks a man holding a gun at face level. Bam! We jump right into the action. We don't know who, what, or why, but you can bet we want to find out. Immediately we're drawn into questions like "What's going on? Who is he? Who is she? Do they know each other? What's with the gun?" And questions, folks, are good things in drama because they imply some sort of dramatic action and subtly seduce an audience into emotionally investing in their answers.

In the previous example, we can find out all of the information about the woman's failing marriage (or the beginning of the play that we don't see) when she suspects the guy with the gun was hired by her husband to kill her. It isn't until the guy with gun is in the apartment for five minutes (or halfway through the play) that the woman in the robe realizes the gunman is at the wrong apartment: she's in apartment 2A; he's looking for the person that lives in 2B.

Look, we only have ten minutes, so let's get it moving and shaking from the get-go. How bad could that be? If you're not comfortable with this idea, and you need something a little more traditional—a true beginning, middle, and end—your conflict has to be articulated in a ten-minute play, I would think, no later than at the end of page 2 or the beginning of page 3 (the actual page numbers are suggestions; there's nothing that exact).

In those first two pages, show us the world we're in, set up your characters, reveal what's at stake for them, and let us watch them behave in the world you've given them. At the end of those first couple of pages, make sure it's absolutely clear what the conflict is (from the previous example, will the woman in the robe get out of this alive?). If you follow traditional structure, you should be so clear about what the conflict is by page 2 that I could get up from my chair, leave the theatre, and tell the first person I see, "It's the story of a group of good-hearted guys who may or may not lose their life savings in the stock market."

Moving forward, we go to pages 3 through 8 or 9, and our goal is to complicate the story in such a way that the audience has no idea how the conclusion will turn out, keeping the dramatic suspense factor high. In the longer, more traditional forms, we might label this Act II, dramatically significant for its multiple complications and rising dramatic action or tension. In a ten-minute play, you have to find the right balance of story complications that can be resolved in the short span of the play. To do so, set your conflict in motion and then complicate the story by (1) introducing other characters who desperately need something themselves and can either help or hinder the central character; (2) introducing unforseen events that alter the course of the story; or (3) letting your central character have a change of heart/mind/soul/gender—anything that will intensify that central dramatic question that begs to be answered.

Obviously, you don't have a lot of time or play-space to outrageously complicate the story in five or six minutes. So my advice is to find one or two complications to the central story that catapult the conflict forward. For example, a young woman longs to regain a connection with her estranged family. When she wins the state lottery and becomes an instant millionaire, she's faced with a real dilemma: Should she tell her perpetually out-of-work, alcoholic father and petty criminal brother that both live in a neighboring town? Will they take advantage of her? Will they reappear in her life for all the wrong reasons? Complication No. 1: the media want her photograph for the area newspaper. Complication No. 2: her boyfriend, who never understood her family dynamic, chides her for being so selfish. Complication No. 3: unaware of her new wealth, the father shows up at her front door, unannounced and drunk.

The last page or so is all about resolution of the conflict and the restoration of a balanced world for the central character. Using the previous example, the young woman's world was relatively balanced when the lights first rose on stage, then quickly became unbalanced when she won the lotto. Her dramatic journey, of course, is to try to restore some sort of emotional balance to her world given the new complication in her life. The last page or so of that play should be about what the young woman will or will not do about sharing her good fortune with her family. Most dramatically pressing is her father, and whatever choice she'll ultimately make (to tell him or not) should be directly affected by what she needs from him: his love; to be left alone; to be loved for what she is and not what she now has; to keep things simply at the status quo.

So to wrap it all up for you in a nice, neat package sans the red bow, if you're writing traditional structure for your ten-minute play, it would look something like this:

Pages 1–2: Set up the world we're in, introduce your central character(s), and make sure we understand what they need/want/desire in the journey of the story.

Pages 2–3: Illuminate the central conflict—a dramatic question that will be answered by the play's end.

Pages 3–8: Complicate the story two or three times.

Pages 9–10: Resolve the conflict, even if that creates an unhappy ending.

3. CREATE INTERESTING DIALOGUE

I know, I know. Easier said than done, right? But in a ten-minute play, every theatrical element counts for something more than in a longer play because we don't have the luxury of time to engage an audience. Every utterance has to count for something, and what better way to define character quickly than through sharp, revealing dialogue?

I don't know if you can truly teach someone to write dialogue, but I do know one thing that makes dialogue for the stage interesting and less ordinary: *No one speaks the same.* I know this may sound simpleminded, but the truth is we often write some sort of generic talk-language in our plays with nothing that identifies the characters. We'd all be better dramatists if, once and for all, we'd acknowledge that no two people speak the same because no two people are the same. We come from different states, countries, cultures, educational backgrounds, family dynamics, political interests, religions, and on and on. Our speech is as unique to us as our fingerprints are, but for some reason we flatten people out when we put them on stage. If you're not sure what I'm talking about, do this simple experiment: Take a page of any play of yours that has more than three characters on it. Using some sort of correction fluid, erase the names of your characters. Now make a photocopy of your page, hand it to a friend, and ask her to identify how many people are talking on the page. If you're like most of my students, you'll be shocked at the answers that come back to you. If you're really daring, try the same experiment with a page that has five or six characters talking on it.

A thirty-five-year-old, rigid academic isn't going to speak the same way a thirty-five-year-old brain surgeon with a highly developed IQ is going to speak, even if they've lived across the hall from each other all their lives. Yes, chances are they're both intelligent, well-read, career-minded people, but something makes them different in their use of language. Maybe the brain surgeon reads comic books in her spare time, watches "Sex in the City" every Sunday night, has never embraced the idea of a nutritional diet, knows the lyrics to every James Taylor tune he ever wrote, and lives to party on the mountain slopes of Colorado. Maybe the rigid academic has a father who is a lawyer, a mother who is a psychiatrist, and for his personal enjoyment, devoutly reads the *Smithsonian* and the *Chronicle of Higher Education* and compulsively watches the Shopping Network. If we put these two people in the same room, they're not going to sound the same.

Your job as a playwright is to listen to, remember, replicate, and imitate how people talk. Some people talk with textbook English; others can barely string three words together in a simple statement. Some people talk in grand images and poetic metaphors; other talk with a saturation of four-letter words. Some people use forty words for one simple idea; others use two words for one complicated idea. Some people use words like *splendiferous*; others use *cool*. Some folks use double negatives ("it ain't no use in tellin' me that"); some use double adjectives ("it was wicked cold"). If you're from New Orleans, you sound different than someone from Boise. If you're shy, you speak one way, and if you're gregarious, another. And beyond the cultural or educational differences in people, if they're nervous, anxious, angry, tired, drunk, happy, or sad, they'll sound even more different. That's what makes us special, individual, unique. So make your characters special, make them different. In a ten-minute play, a writer can tell me loads about a person through the way he or she speaks, leaving more stage time to develop the story and plot points.

4. USE YOUR SENSE OF THE THEATRICAL

That, of course, assumes that you have a sense of the theatrical. If you don't, think about this: What makes theatre, theatre? What can you do in theatre that you can't do on television or film? What do live actors bring to the occasion? An audience? A director's vision? If we see an actor literally fly across the stage, why is it more special in a theatre than if we see an actor do the same thing in a film? Keep asking yourself: what makes theatre, theatre? Those Greeks used a chorus for something; Brecht got in your face for some reason; Chekhov made you wait endlessly for some purpose. And it all has to do with that which is inherently theatrical, that which requires a live audience to experience the thrill of live performance guided by your thoughts as a writer, your ideas, and your sense of creating worlds that we ordinarily don't see, or at least don't see from your perspective.

Break out of the box and consider setting your play on the wing of an airplane (if it's appropriate). Have a modern-day chorus of three cab drivers report Rachel's journey to the Big Apple. Have your characters engage the audience, pitch ball to the audience, hell, serve burgers to the audience if it makes sense to the storytelling of your play. Underscore that serious confrontational scene between mother and daughter with an inexplicable baby's cry in the distance. Make the light so bright it's blinding when the building contractor finally comes clean with his dirty business deals. Flood the stage with exaggerated sounds of a business office over the wedding scene or the sound of a clock incessantly ticking if it serves the idea you're exploring.

Open your imagination to what the theatre can provide. Remember, we can isolate and amplify light, sound, and people. We can tell our audience where to look and control how long they hold their gaze. We can paint the world solid blue with one red dot hanging mysteriously in the air. Or, we can create a realistic booth in a diner that's as interesting as any of the above. As my colleague Michael Wright has said many times before in his books on playwriting, "Remember, playwriting is Play At Writing."

5. BE SPECIFIC

There is nothing more glorious to an audience than to be seduced by specific, imagistic writing. If you're telling a new friend about the house you grew up in, obviously the more specific you are about the color of the house, the expanse of the front yard, the crooked, cracked driveway, and the tree you climbed on summer nights, the better chance he has of appreciating your emotional recollection and memory. If as a playwright, you want me to understand that one of your characters has just completed a road trip across the country, then you can add to my enjoyment of the tale if your character tells me the trip was made in an aqua blue '67 Thunderbird convertible that he bought from a retired World War II veteran who cried the day he sold it.

Your character can tell me the road trip was "great fun," or he can tell me "the only time I remember having that much fun was when my dad and I got lost in Yosemite National Park for three days with two Japanese tourists who knew four words in English: *hello*, *good-bye*, and *bathroom*, *please*." He can tell me "The car drove great," or he can say, "The car glided down the highway like it was skating on ice." The more specific you are in your writing, the larger the world you create for me. Without knowing it, I'm in your world, fully participating in my imagination, and all you did was draw me in with the help a few specific words. And if I'm going to be in your world for such a short time, let me see it from every angle you can think of.

6. WORRY ABOUT WHAT'S TOO MUCH

An explanation by way of a painful example: I was working somewhere away from New York and was invited to a showcase of ten-minute plays centered around the theme "What Would You Say if You Finally Had the Chance to Say It?" Oy vey. Before I ever got there I knew I was in big trouble.

What appeared on stage was a series of ten-minute plays in which the central characters finally got to say to whomever what they'd always wanted to say about some past injury, insult, disappointment, or heartache. And because the writers were for the most part inexperienced (at least I hope that was the excuse), what we were treated to was two hours of people ranting about everything—and I do mean *everything*—that ever pissed them off about another person. Each play started with the central character just addressing one issue connected to the other person, but inevitably grew to an out-and-out indictment of every ill of their relationship. It was exhausting, frustrating, . . . and uninteresting. Why?

First, the theme, which of course appeared in print, tipped off the audience to the central dramatic action. We knew there was going to be a car wreck and we were just waiting to see when it was going to happen and if somebody were going to lose a head or an arm. Secondly, and most important, almost all of the writers saturated the ten minutes with so many issues between the two people that it left me to wonder, "How in the hell are they going to resolve all of that in such a short amount of time?" Silly me. What was I thinking? There was no resolution, just a hefty ol' dose of "Good! I feel better now that I've gotten that off my chest." Finally, and don't ask me why or how this happened, hardly any of the secondary characters ever got a chance for a rebuttal. They had to just sit there and take it! Later I thought, that was actually a good thing, because if they had started in with their issues about the main characters, my head would have exploded.

The scope of what you write has to fit inside that very small ten-minute container. Granted, there has to be conflict that is resolved to some sort of audience satisfaction. But if you top-load the play with too many character issues—her brother hates her; her sister steals from her; the landlord's threatening to sue her for her back rent; and she didn't get accepted to the college of her choice—either you're writing a farce, where compound issues are essential, or you're teetering on melodrama. If you're writing about a relationship that's ending between two people, let it be ending because of one or two painful, irreconcilable differences between them, not twenty.

"But I know people like that. I know relationships that have that many problems," I can hear some of you saying. Fine. Get them all to a therapist. But don't put them on stage as characters unless you're making a very intelligent, very purposeful comment about their life situation. An audience that has too much to care about or invest in often ends up caring about nothing because it's simply too overwhelming in such a short amount of time.

7. AVOID THE PARK BENCH PLAY

Question (or a joke, depending on your perspective): How many of the short plays ever written have been set in a park on a bench? Answer: Too many. Too friggin' many. So many that if I never saw another, I'd be a happier man. And for some reason, a short play seems to beg of its writer to be set on a park bench. There are so many more interesting places that two people can happen upon one another: a baseball game, divorce court, at confession, at a bar mitzvah, at an art auction, a funeral, a tennis game, a pig wrestling competition—just about anywhere you can imagine. Ahhh, there's the AOL key word: *imagine*. Use your imagination and get off the park bench unless you really need a park to serve the play.

8. THE "F" WORD

Okay, relax. I'm not going to say don't use it. I'm not even going to suggest how often you use it. I will say this: if you didn't use the "f" word, what would be in its place? Just think about it sometime. Yeah, I know: people talk like that. A lot of people talk like that. I sometimes talk like that. But when I do, it's because other people around me are talking like that, or they expect me to talk like that, or I'm trying to fit in, or stand out, or sound hip, or sound younger than I am. As a writer, wouldn't it be more dramatically interesting if you could find a good behavioral reason to use the "f" word instead of just using it as phonetic comma?

9. PLAY THE FORMAT GAME

Absolutely, undeniably, without a shadow of a doubt, make a cover page for your play with the title, your name, and contact information. A second page should follow that is devoted to a character breakdown, listing each character's name, sex, age, and any physical, emotional, or relationship information we need to know prior to seeing the play: "Naomi, F., 25: tall, brittle, angry; mother of twins." Also on this page, you can provide for us the time and location of the story: "New York City, Upper West Side tenement building, 1972." These two pages *do not* count in the overall page numbers of your play, so don't sweat it and do do it. Number the first page of dialogue as page 1. When you don't do this, and you put all of that contact and character information on your first page of dialogue, you're eating up valuable space. And there are a lot of theatres that systematically don't read plays that go beyond that tenth page in number.

10. KNOW THAT YOU DON'T HAVE TO AGREE WITH OR COMPLETELY UNDERSTAND TIPS 1–9 TO WRITE A GOOD PLAY

Look, all of this information comes from my experiences of writing and teaching for a lot of years. I take this stuff from the mistakes I've made and mistakes I've seen other people make and from watching how other writers succeed in the theatre. I've tried to share with you some valuable lessons I've learned the hard way, but it may not hit you in any kind of meaningful way. So take what I've suggested that resonates for you, let it work its way into your creative psyche, and then write your ten-minute play the way you want to write it. If you find you're not making the mark in your own definition of success, reread tips 1–9 and see if they make any more sense to you. If they do, good. If they don't, keep writing. You'll figure it out.

And if all else fails, read the next chapter about how to figure out if you're sabotaging your own writing.

3
CHAPTER

Dear Abby: My Ten-Minute Play Sucks. Why?

With any limitation in the theatre, there is immense creative freedom. A whole explosion of creativity is going to open up when you limit the story of your play to an elevator. But if you put the world of your play in the middle of Grand Central Station, it's less interesting.

—Laura Margolis, Producing Manager, StageWorks

SOMETIMES WRITERS, MYSELF INCLUDED, ARE JUST BIG, FAT, sloppy, snotty-nosed, sticky-fingered babies. We don't want someone to tell us what to do! We don't want someone telling us how to create our art! We don't want someone to put us in a playpen and say, "You can only play in here, in this square. Not out there. Not over there. In here. Just here." But when we're writing ten-minute plays, let's acknowledge one simple fact: a human being—usually a harried producer—actually has to *produce* the play you've written. Hello? Slap yourself in the face and wake up for this. *Someone has to actually* produce *the play you've written.* And regardless of any argument you or I can make about artistic freedom or artistic expression, someone has to translate your written word to a visual representation on stage. So be smart, and avoid having to write that "Dear Abby: My ten-minute play sucks. And it feels like nobody loves me. Why?" letter.

When a producer is organizing an evening of ten-minute plays, he or she has to consider his or her resources—money, directors, actors, rehearsal time, tech time, technical limitations, publicity—in relation to the number of playwrights being produced. On the most basic level, eight playwrights equals eight plays equals eight mini-productions. Therefore, it only makes sense that we make our plays attractive not only dramatically but also production-wise. If we construct our plays in such a way that they mean one less production headache for the producer, our chances of getting produced aren't guaranteed, but they're better than at least 50 percent of the others. Consider a recent experience I had:

I was producing a ten-minute play festival for an Off-Off Broadway theatre in New York that had no wing space, no fly space, a small room backstage that could fit five, maybe six Calista Flockharts shoulder to shoulder, and a few technical necessities—your typical underfunded, overstressed New York black box. A young woman submitted a play that I thought was absolutely brilliant—a word I rarely use to describe someone's writing. There was only one small problem: the text called for a flying bicycle. That's right. A bicycle that magically flew across the space, back and forth, up and down. You couldn't do the play without the image of the flying bicycle, so of course, I couldn't produce the play, and it broke my heart. I called the writer to tell her how much I liked the play, but that I couldn't produce the piece because of the inherent technical problem in the text. She said, "Gosh, I never thought about that."

Think about it. I'm begging you. I'm pleading with you! Don't break my heart by writing a play I'll love but can't possibly produce. Here are ten things I believe you can leave out of your work when you write. If you do, maybe we'll meet each other one day when I call to say, "Congratulations, we'd like to produce your play."

1. THE SETTING FROM HELL: THE PRODUCER'S POINT OF VIEW

Don't set your play in the kitchen of a four-star restaurant that requires three ovens, two stoves, five waiters, and two dueling chefs preparing a full dinner for the president of the United States. Remember, there's a producer behind this production, and he or she is counting bucks, people power, favors owed, and hours in the day to produce not just your play but six or seven others. It takes money to have all that stuff. It takes technicians to drag it on and off the stage. It takes time to drag it on and off the stage, more time than an evening of ten-minute plays can afford.

I know you think a dorm room's just a dorm room—nothing fancy there. But if you're writing realism, then that dorm room has to have beds, a table, chairs, books, computers, posters, and vomit stains on the carpet from that miserable frat boy who blew chunks in the room on a drunken Saturday night. So be smart. Note in the text, "A dorm room represented by a table, a chair, a computer, and a 'Go Cardinals!' poster for the Lamar University football team." Let someone know that you've thought of an easy way to establish the setting of your play that won't give the designers a nervous breakdown.

2. THE SETTING FROM HELL: THE DESIGNER'S POINT OF VIEW

Don't set your play on the front porch of a two-story, restored Victorian house that we're supposed to see both the inside and upstairs of. Remember, there's a production stage manager and set designer behind this production, not to mention a limited budget, and they have to design a space that eight different plays can work in and that can be changed or rearranged with ease and speed. Your play does not stand alone; it has to fit within the context of an evening of plays.

I know I told you to think out of the box, and I still want you to do that. But be reasonable in your thinking. Here's my own personal, secret formula. Before I set my ten-minute plays anywhere I say to myself, "If I had to build the set of my play all by my lonesome self, where would I set the play?" Chances are you may find yourself in just that position. God knows I have. And you really don't want me anywhere near a hammer and nails and certainly no power tools. So the simpler the better. Everyone will thank you.

3. THE CAST FROM HELL

Don't have a dancing sailor chorus of fifteen; make it three, tops, if that many. If you do that, you've got those three, the captain, the captain's girlfriend, the captain's girlfriend's boyfriend, his lover, his lover's father, and his lover's father's parrot (I know, it can be the stage manager dressed in green garbage bags and a smart yellow cap, but he still has to be counted). Okay, that's a total of nine people in ten pages. Wheeeewww! That's a lot of folks in a little time. And can you really get an actor to do the part of the captain when all he does is limp on stage with an oak branch as a cane, look at the dancing sailor chorus, and say, "Velveeta, anyone?" It's not impossible, but I think it'd be a hard sell to a producer that you actually need nine people for your short, ten-minute play, especially since one of those characters has only one line. Also, and I know this shouldn't be a real consideration, but . . . trying to juggle the lives of nine actors, one director, one writer, one stage manager, and other technicians can be a nightmare. You might as well be doing *Angels in America, Parts I and II*, for all of that effort.

4. AND 5. THE TECH FROM HELL

Don't have (4.) thirty sound cues, (5a.) fifty-two light cues, or (5b.) eight changes of costume unless you want to see a very haggard and intensely cranky technical crew. Remember, there are technicians behind this production that have to punch the buttons, pull the levers, time the fadeouts, score the music up, shoot the gun off, pull the shoes off while putting the shirt on, and strike the tin sheet for the lightning effect. And aesthetically, if you overburden your ten-minute play with technical requirements, it could look and sound more like a video clip from the "People's Choice Awards" than a play.

Since your work is not a stand-alone play, the lighting designer has to use all lighting instruments for all plays. Maybe she can give you one isolated spotlight center stage, but I guarantee you she can't give you eight isolated spots. The costume designer has to work with a number of casts and costume requirements, usually begging, borrowing, or stealing where she can to costume actors. A sound designer, if you're fortunate enough to have one, has to make, cue, re-cue, and instruct the board operator for every sound cue in the whole evening, not just your play.

Now, having said all of that, don't be afraid to fill the world of your play with what you feel is thematically or dramatically necessary. But do consider every technical requirement as one small piece of a much, much larger pie.

6. THE WRITER FROM HELL

Don't think that the label "ten-minute play" could possibly apply to your fifteen minutes of work. Wouldn't it be a drag to get a call from an artistic director who says he'd love to do your play if you'd consider cutting five minutes out of it? In the longer form, that's the equivalent of cutting Act I from a three-act play. Playwrights for some reason haven't grasped the concept that ten minutes means ten minutes, not twelve, and certainly not fifteen. All those "it's only eleven/twelve/thirteen minutes" arguments are a real crock. Consider this: if a producer has your play, and it's fifteen minutes, and she's got seven others that clock in at fifteen minutes, you're looking at an evening of ten-minute plays that should be eighty minutes total plus intermission, but is in reality one hundred and twenty minutes plus intermission. Add in scene changes, and it's beginning to look like a very long evening of theatre.

Here's another problem with cheating the minute thing: audiences know that what they're watching is supposed to be a ten-minute play. When a play starts to clock in around twelve or thirteen minutes, the audience (myself included) starts thinking, "This isn't ten minutes. This isn't even twelve minutes." But even more important than that, your audience has stopped paying attention to your play.

Playwrights are stubborn. They don't want to accept the limitation of the form and instead try to find ways to trick the producer's eye—smaller fonts, larger margins. We're not that blind, ya'll. We see what you're doing. And even if your play has the magical number 10 on the last page, don't think this means that it's ten minutes long (because we don't). So do the hard-boiled egg thing and time it! That's right. Sit down, read it out loud, and time the damn thing. That way you're sure, and you'll never get that "cut it" phone call.

7.–9. THREE WAYS TO CHEAT THE SYSTEM THAT DON'T WORK AND DO MAKE YOU LOOK BAD

When I see the following on the physical page in a ten-minute play, I know exactly the kind of writer I'm dealing with. Don't do this to yourself; don't do it to me. I want to like you, not ignore you. When you change the size of your typeface (bad move No. 7) so you can cram fourteen pages into ten, I can see that like the flashing neon sign it is. Your script should be printed in a twelve-point font. When you expand the margins from the usual one-inch parameter toward the edges of the page (bad move No. 8) to a half-inch to fit more script in, I can see this like a billboard in my front yard. When you shrink the spacing between character names, dialogue, and stage directions (bad move No. 9) to fit more script in, I can see that like a car driving through my kitchen window. It's that obvious.

10. THE DANGLING THIRD

It's your call, but when you write ten pages and a third, there are some theatres that will throw your script in the trash. For many producing organizations, the only way they can ensure some consistency in the time factor—though I'm not really convinced it works—is to make a hard-and-fast rule that if it's longer than ten pages, it can't be considered for production. You may see this as silly, but they see it as practical. So, yeah, I know, it's just five lines on page 11, but for some producers, that's five lines too many.

I've been there. I know what it's like to not want to cut those five lines just to get it to page 10. So do this: Look through the script to see if there are any stage directions or parenthetical actor directions that can be eliminated. Is there any repetitive dialogue? Is there a whole dramatic beat that can be shortened or cut altogether? Can you combine sections of one character's dialogue and streamline what he says? Give it a shot; see what happens.

Look, I'm for anything that gets writers writing and theatres exposed to more voices. But a ten-minute play will go where? Most likely in a ten-minute play festival for the Theatre Behind the Bowling Alley because (1) they're relatively easy to produce, (2) audiences are treated to a diversity of voices, (3) they're great opportunities for actors, (4) they're a terrific challenge for designers, and (5) theatres are introduced to a number of new playwrights they can nurture and cultivate relationships with.

At NYU, I produce our annual Ten-Minute Play Festival, and here's what I have to play with: a rectangular stage area twenty-five feet wide by seventeen feet deep, in other words, tiny; a ceiling that is twelve feet high with a light grid that can barely keep the lighting instruments off the heads of the audience members; barely four feet of backstage area; no wings, no sides, no teasers, no curtains; no green room for the actors; a regulation door that functions as an emergency exit at the lip of the stage; and no costume or prop storage. All of those conditions have a profound effect on what I can reasonably produce in that space. I don't want to make myself or my actors, directors, and technicians miserable and, perhaps most importantly, disappoint a writer because I couldn't serve the vision of his or her play. And just so you know, our theatre is not unlike a good number of the smaller theatres in this country. My situation of fitting the play to the space is hardly uncommon.

So, if you're going to write in this genre, write so you'll be produced. Otherwise, what's the point?

4

CHAPTER

Serious Murder on Your Mind

PROBLEMS IN PRODUCTION
AND THE PEOPLE WHO CAUSE THEM

Sometimes the set is just a door . . . I'm one to keep it as simple as possible.

—B. J. Scott, Artistic Director, Camino Real Playhouse

IF YOU'RE A WRITER, DON'T TURN THE PAGE BECAUSE YOU THINK this doesn't apply to you. Everything about your art, including its production, applies to you. So hunker down, read on, and appreciate what has to happen to create even the smallest world for a ten-minute play. If you're an artistic director, producer, or stage manager, read this as the gospel it is, 'cause, ohhh, mercy, I've had to learn the hard way.

I produced my first ten-minute play festival seven years ago (and lived to tell the story). Even though I'd produced a hundred or so one-act and full-length plays, never, *never* could I have predicted the quicksand-as-art that I would experience with the ten-minute. Never mind that I am compulsively organized; forget that I have lots more resources than most small theatres; fuhgettabout the small army that I always have working with me—because nothing could have prepared me for what was ahead. Okay, I admit: part of the problem was my own blind ignorance, but a good part of the problem is the nature of the beast—there's just a helluva lot going on in a very small amount of time with tons of people everywhere. What's more, producing a group of ten-minute plays year to year is production-unique because each year there's a different kind of struggle with each new group of playwrights, plays, directors, and actors. So sit back and learn from someone who's been there, done that, and sold the leftover T-shirts on the street corner.

1. FORCING A SIZE 12 FOOT INTO A SIZE 4 SHOE

Let's say, for the sake of discussion, you're producing eight ten-minute plays for one evening's worth of theatre and that you're going to run that evening four days a week for three weeks (a standard Equity showcase code contract). No matter how you slice it, Chef, you're producing eight different plays with eight different casts and directors. And even though they're ten minutes long, they might as well each be a full-length play for all the work that you're going to put into them.

What will make you or break you is technical support staff. You *need* an efficient, hardworking staff that can accommodate the sheer volume of people—and egos—involved. When I produce our annual festival at NYU, that translates to eight directors, one set designer, one lighting designer, one costumer designer, one production stage manager (PSM), two assistant stage managers (ASMs), and a crackerjack running crew (lights, sound, and backstage) of at least three or four people. I can almost hear you gulp. I'm not suggesting that you have to have all of these folks in place. There are some people, however, that are just plain indispensable.

You can never have too many hands in a production like this, and you need one lone person to be in charge of them all. You *need* a PSM beyond the individual stage manager(s) for any one play. Why? Traffic. Lots of it. Loads o' people—everywhere. You need one responsible, attempting-to-be-calm person in charge who won't be trapped for hours at any one play's rehearsal, someone at home base who can see and understand the big picture and organize it.

The PSM will schedule all of your production meetings, follow up on that endless list of production details that grows larger as time passes, serve as the liaison between the designers and the directors, coordinate rehearsal schedules and dress rehearsals—in effect, function as the director of the evening. More important, this person schedules and executes that maddening technical weekend or week prior to opening, wherein eight different casts with a pile of directors descend on the theatre to set technical cues. Someone has to stay on the clock to keep everyone sane and focused; a competent PSM can do that and more.

I assign four plays each to my two ASMs. They attend rehearsals, record blocking, keep the production book, shop for simple stage props, take notes—all the standard responsibilities of a stage manger. They also report weekly to the PSM. The single biggest problem the ASMs have to work through, whether they're covering two plays or five, is often needing to be in different places at the same time because of the different rehearsal schedules. At NYU, it'd be nice if I had eight stage managers, one for each play, but I don't and never will because I can barely afford the two. So it requires everyone—primarily the directors—to coordinate his or her efforts to accommodate the ASMs. The only other solution is to do away with the ASMs altogether and have the directors perform some of the basic stage manager functions—not the ideal situation, but workable.

In production, the ASMs are in the light and sound booth calling the show, usually rotating their efforts every other play. This keeps them fresh and alert. In situations where I don't have ASMs, my PSM attends enough rehearsals to understand the flow of each play then brings the show into tech weekend and calls each show from the booth. It can work, but it can also age that PSM years ahead of his or her time because he or she is responsible for everything from when an actor shows up at the theatre to that final light cue at the end of the evening. And of course, whatever she or he does for one play, she or he does for eight.

Your running crews—the most underappreciated people in the theatre—have to be some of the most dedicated, committed, and diligent workers you can find. Whatever you do, don't give this area of the production over to the slackers hanging around your theatre. I've made this mistake, thinking, "How bad could it be?" Trust me, it's a nightmare, because these folks have to change sets, set props, repatch dimmers, quick-change an actor, and cue the stage manager in less than a minute. Multiply all of this by eight in one evening just for each play's preshow, let alone what happens in the interior and at the conclusion of each play, and you can appreciate the job that's in front of them. You need a group of team players who operate together like a finely oiled piece of machinery and who aren't eating Captain Crunch out of the box while listening to techno-house music on their headphones.

I know this sounds like an awful lot of people working on what should be a relatively simple production, and you're right, it is. But don't try to put a size 12 foot in a size 4 shoe. Better to be overstaffed than understaffed, particularly if it's your first time doing it. If you've got favors due you in the community, put the call out. In this kind of production, you won't be sorry to see so many people working together toward the common good. You'll be left to produce and promote the show with a clear, thinking head, and you might have only five sleepless nights instead of fifteen.

2. BOTTLENECKING: FIFTY ACTORS OR FIVE

If you're doing eight plays, you can count on casting at least sixteen actors (two actors per play), minimum. When some plays require three, four, or five characters, your casting needs multiply. There are two ways to approach casting, and your choice ultimately rests with how you need to serve the artists connected to your company. If you have ten or so actors that make up the core of your acting company, you can cast actors in multiple roles from different plays. This can be a good thing for several reasons: (1) actors are challenged by trying to define a variety of character types; (2) actors get to showcase their wide range of skill; (3) there are less people for your PSM to keep track of; (4) if you have limited dressing room space or backstage space, there are less people to juggle and fewer incidents of elbows to eyeballs; and (5) an audience gets a genuine kick out of seeing one actor transform for several different, often difficult roles.

But there are some downsides to multiple casting that will give you (or someone) a big ol' mutha of a headache if you're not careful. There are eight plays that require eight different rehearsal schedules. You can't fault a director for believing his or her rehearsal is the most important, and understandably the directors want all of their actors at their rehearsals at all times. When you cast an actor in three or four different plays, there's got to be a lot of preplanning or you'll have a lot of angry people on your hands if you can't assure everyone of some quality time with one another.

Also, actors who attend a lot of different rehearsals are stretching their valuable time to begin with; rehearsals, coupled with working, studying for school, maintain relationships, and so on, leaves very little room for anything else. Actors need free-head time to work on their characters—something I know I've been guilty of forgetting in the past. They need preparation time; hell, they need some just good ol' downtime. If we treat them like cattle, they'll behave like cattle. Finally, you should at least consider that an actor cast in three or four roles has to labor through hours and hours of technical rehearsals, eating up his energy at a time his needs it the most. And just remember: when any one of us gets overly tired, that's when we stop doing our jobs well; in the theatre, that's when those ugly diva alter egos rear their ugly heads.

If you have a large number of actors you want to serve, or if you just want to get to know a large pool of actors in a relatively safe venture, casting single actors for single roles in a festival of ten-minute plays is an ideal situation. Everyone wins: your directors will thank you because they don't have to negotiate rehearsal schedules with one another; you get to see a wide spectrum of talent to consider for your future productions; your audience numbers increase because each actor invites a group of friends; and there's more people to help build the set, strike the set, scout for props, and promote the evening.

The downside to single-role casting is obvious: bottlenecking everywhere. Do you have enough dressing room space? Green room space? Backstage space? Where do you put twenty-four actors? How can you accommodate their needs prior to a performance (physical and vocal warm-ups)? How do you accommodate their needs during a performance? Do they take their curtain calls after their individual performances and then leave the theatre, or do you draw everyone involved together at the end of Act I for their bows, then Act II? Or do you have a full company bow at the end of Act II? And if you do that, are you prepared to have twenty-four actors hanging out for two hours until the curtain call? Do you limit everyone's playbill biographies to fifty words so that the program doesn't look like a phone book?

These are all very real and practical considerations that with some preplanning and thought shouldn't be an issue. But you do have to think about them, and better sooner than later.

3. EIGHT CAN FEEL LIKE EIGHTY

Do eight plays mean eight directors? Your call. Economics, people resources, and time to find, hire, and orient them to your theatre are certainly all considerations. It's eight additional people to deal with, and with so many people already involved, eight more people can feel like eighty. Regardless of how you configure the director thing, keep this in mind: the more directors you have, the more effort will be required to schedule rehearsals that don't conflict in the limited rehearsal space you have. There will be much more time spent negotiating and compromising between your designers and directors to accommodate eight unique visions of the individual plays. And on a purely administrative level, it's more difficult to work around eight people's personal lives to schedule a production meeting than it is with four. Still, it's a great venue to see the work of eight different directors whom you're considering for larger, longer work in your theatre.

4. DESIGNER MAYHEM

The scenic and lighting designers will have murder and mayhem on their minds if you don't allow them to conceptualize the evening of work using a unit set and repertory light plot. Trying to accommodate eight locations for eight very different plays interpreted through the eyes of different directors becomes a logistical nightmare. The design challenge is to integrate the individuality of each play into the working whole, and it's been my experience that the designers welcome that challenge over the alternative of trying to create eight unique environments.

If you incorporate the idea of a unit set—one environment that all plays must function in—the scenic designer's job is to make the look of the space interesting and suitable for all eight plays and functional for their action. The most successful scenic designs I've seen are those that are not specific to any kind of realistic interior or exterior but are instead more of an open space in which the parameters are defined by the strategic placement of platforms, flats, and some furniture. I don't know enough about design to suggest anything more concrete, but I do know that a booth at a diner, the front row of a movie theatre, the bow of a boat, the front seat of a car, a rocky crag in Scotland, and an attendant's desk at a funeral home are all very real possibilities in the world of these plays. Simple, identifying set pieces that move in and out of the stage space freely and, most importantly, quickly, are oftentimes all you need to distinguish the location.

I've seen a harried producer/artistic director (and admittedly have done this myself) face a group of directors and writers and say, "Look, you have four chairs, two tables, a park bench, two platforms, and a bookshelf with which to make this work." It's not the ideal situation—what if the play is set on a sandy beach?—but oftentimes, that's truly all you have because of limited budgets and personnel. Use what you have, but find someone with a creative eye to take those four chairs, two tables, the park bench, the platforms, and the bookshelf and apply a unifying paint treatment or texture to them as well as the floors and walls. You want to try to avoid that "we just pulled this out of our garage" look because most audiences want a heightened theatrical atmosphere and not something that looks like what they park their Volvo next to every night. Like I said to the playwrights, limitations should force you to be more creative, not less.

What a scenic designer can't completely provide in terms of the individuality of each play, a lighting designer can. Every theatre has its own technical limitations, but if it's possible, allow your lighting designer to provide each play its own look, its own visual environment that will support the world of the play. You might have only twenty feet by twenty feet of actual performance space, but with a very creative lighting designer, that space can be made to look like twenty different places, which is just what you need when you're changing locales so often and quickly. If your resources are limited (and whose aren't, really), a standard repertory light plot plus a few strategically placed "specials" can provide enough of a difference to trick the eye into believing there's been a change in locations.

Your biggest headache when creating the performance environment is a people/artistic problem. What works aesthetically for one director or one writer will often not work for another. One director will tell you that the wide, open space your designer has created is perfect for his or her rocky crag in Scotland; another director will tell you that the space is too open to create the intimacy needed for the bedroom play. If you're dealing with talented designers, these problems can be solved easily enough. But many of us don't always have the luxury of true designers with well-stocked resources. My suggestion then falls to the writer: make sure we understand where we are in your play by what you say in your play; the audience members will fill in the gap. They're cooperative that way.

5. THE TIME NAZI

None of us has enough time—ever. It's never our friend. If I could balance my laptop in one hand while writing this and stir a pot of chili for supper with the other, I'd do it, because I never have enough time to do it all. And when you're producing a ten-minute play festival, time is the big enemy that everyone, in their zealousness to create, forgets. The writers are convinced that their plays are ten minutes, regardless of the fact that they're clocking in at thirteen, fourteen, and sixteen minutes. That's when you begin hearing, "If Brandon would only pick up his pace in Scene 1, the play would come in right on time." (Hello? Three minutes' worth?) Because of these writers' shortsightedness, what the producer thinks is going to be an evening of ninety minutes will undoubtedly stretch to two hours. In performance, your audience members are then aware of the time because they thought they were coming to see eight ten-minute plays and they've done the simple math.

Directors get caught up in their rehearsals and forget that there is another director and cast outside the rehearsal hall waiting to start their rehearsal. The director outside is steaming because she knows she's only got two hours before she loses her principal actor to another rehearsal. When the door opens between the two directors, they grumble and shoot each other nasty eye-daggers.

Tech days are a nightmare because the producer insists, in order to keep everyone sane, that each play gets only three hours of total tech time—a total of twenty-four straight working hours for the technicians. The technicians think it's too much; the directors, not enough. Publicity people get frazzled because there are twenty-nine people in the company and only half have turned in their program biographies on time. The sound guy can't figure out for the life of him why one of the ten-minute plays has twenty-six sound cues and is frantically scurrying to get them all recorded and cued. At the end of the day, no one is satisfied; everyone goes home cranky. What to do?

Nothing. There's nothing you can do, except make everyone aware of how crucial it is that all involved respect time from every angle and treat it like the illusive burglar it is. To that end, one of the smartest lessons I've learned over the years is to hold an all-company meeting before anyone goes into rehearsal. Invited is every human being working on the project. We sit, discuss, and outline the effort at hand. That's when I introduce myself as the Time Nazi and warn everyone—writers, directors, designers—about staying on the clock. Then I can be a hard-ass when need be, because I've warned them. If I need the plays, for example, to come in on the ten-minute mark, and I've told the writer *early on*, "Cut it or we'll drop it," then I can do just that and walk away with a clear conscience.

6. THE PLAYBILL AS PHONE BOOK

When it comes to programs and publicity for your ten-minute plays, there can be names and biographies that would go on for days. Publicity postcards can look like a page out of your local phone book if you try to cite everyone involved. The program can be practically unreadable because you've shrunk the font so small to fit in everyone's biography. What I've done in the past to solve the problem is workable: In the program and on the postcard/poster, list only the writer, directors, and designers. Inside the program, the tech staff (including designers), directors, and writers have biographies. On a wall outside the theatre, we post all of the actors' photographs (sometimes forty plus) and place a handsomely typed biography in a readable font just below each photograph. The audience then has something to look at during the preshow and intermission. If your actors don't have headshots, grab a disposable camera and have some fun.

7. HELLO? IS ANYBODY OUT THERE? THE DISAPPEARING AUDIENCE

I've tried everything I can think of to solve this problem, but people are people and whether we like it or not, a lot of the audience members are there only to see their friends. Once they see them, they leave and often don't wait until an intermission to do so. This makes me really crazy, especially when I have to turn people away at the door who genuinely want to see the whole evening. And even though those that leave have paid full price for a ticket, they're still leaving the theatre half-empty for a group of actors to play to. Too many times I've seen the theatre jammed to the walls for Act I and watched the audience empty out at the intermission, leaving four people to see Act II. But what can you do?

Two things: At the beginning of the show we make an announcement that it's unsafe for audience members to leave their seats in the dark during the show (true) and ask that they make every effort to wait until intermission. We also tell our actors who will be appearing in Act II to tell their friends that if they can't secure a ticket for the top of the show, to come back to the theatre on the intermission and we'll let them in for half-price. Neither of these things solves the problem entirely, but it does cut down on some of the traffic in and out of the theatre and provides some sort of audience for Act II.

8. LONG PLAY'S JOURNEY INTO NIGHT

I included ten plays in the first festival of ten-minute plays I produced, thinking that it sounded cool to promote "Ten by Ten." The evening started at 8:05 and concluded at 10:40. No one was more surprised than me—unhappily so, I might add.

Everyone is fooled by the label "ten-minute play." It sounds short, and in fact, it should be short. But even if you have eight ten-minute plays that clock in right on time, that's eighty minutes. Add a minute changeover between plays (even that's too long), and you're at eighty-seven minutes. Add a ten-minute intermission and now you're at ninety-seven minutes. Add five more minutes when you hold at the top of the show for late arrivals: a hundred and two minutes. Add five more minutes because not everyone could cycle through the bathrooms at intermission: a hundred and seven minutes. Now add two more plays because you think "they're only ten minutes": a hundred and twenty-seven minutes. Now add five more minutes for the unforseen: a hundred and thirty-two minutes, or two hours and twelve minutes. Now you're producing something that's beginning to feel like *Long Day's Journey into Night*.

9. LET THE MUSIC PLAY

Preshow and postshow music have become standard practice in lot of our theatre productions. In a ten-minute play festival, it becomes a problem because each director who wants music is understandably concerned only about its appropriateness to his or her play. The problem arises when the tune that's playing at the end of one play isn't appropriate to the play that follows. "Easy," you say, "just fade one song out and the other up to start the next play." True, but if you're playing music at the beginning or end of a play, you have to play enough of the music to create the effect you desire, and the time between plays becomes longer and longer.

My solution is really simple: no director can provide preshow or post-show music for individual plays. I use instrumental music between each play to bridge the transitions. It's less complicated and works just as well.

10. DO UNTO OTHERS . . . THE EXACT SAME WAY

Our most valuable resource in the theatre is people. We depend on the goodwill of those we work with to make our experiences personally satisfying and artistically rewarding. Naturally, we want everyone to feel appreciated and respected as much as we want it for ourselves. You know what your own strengths and weaknesses are as an administrator, a director, a producer, or an artistic director. What you may not be aware of is how your best intentions can create a storm of resentment and anger.

If you allow one playwright to write beyond the ten-minute mark, be prepared to do the same for all. If you turn your head the other way when one director exceeds his or her tech time by an hour, know that you'll have seven other directors who expect you to do the same for them. Look, we're human. We want to be treated fairly and equally. And when it looks like someone is getting preferential treatment, bad feelings grow like wildfire, and you can kiss the idea of "ensemble" good-bye. And that becomes just the beginning of your problems . . .

Ten-minute plays are a real kick in the pants when they're done well. But let's go forward into the new millennium with a clear head about it: shorter doesn't mean easier on any level, and they're harder to produce than any of us thinks. When you produce them, think of it as a big, complicated musical—a kind of *Sunset Boulevard* meets the Radio City Music Hall Rockettes has an affair with Edward Albee, and you'll begin to appreciate what it takes to get that goat up on its feet.

5

CHAPTER

To Avoid Humiliation on Ice

ADVICE FROM THOSE WHO KNOW

The conflict's there—it's just hidden.

Yes! I know, I know. It's eighteen minutes, but I took all the "pauses" out and see, the actors don't act any faster.

I didn't know it was supposed to be just ten pages . . . honest. I heard it could be, like, twenty pages if you have a really good director.

—Three of the silliest comments I've ever heard
from playwrights about their ten-minute plays

EVER TRIED TO ICE-SKATE? REMEMBER THE FIRST TIME YOU DID? I do. In two seconds this Texas boy was down for the count, my legs split in opposite directions: one leg pointing to Los Angeles and the other pointing due east, to New York. My face had carved about a half-inch slice into the ice. My first thought was "Shit, that hurts." My second thought was "Who saw me do that?" My third thought was "Why didn't I let her teach me a few things before I got on the ice?" My final thought was "You're always too eager. You always jump in feet first. Could you once just wait and listen to a little simple advice?"

I think I'm a pretty smart guy. But when it comes to my writing, I always assume there are many other people so much brighter and smarter than me because they've been doing it longer, harder, and with more thought. I've learned that if you're really smart, you figure out early on how to connect with those smarter than you and learn from their experiences. Everybody's got a different story to tell, a different perspective, and it's all valuable to you.

I thought I'd try to save you the ice-skating humiliation and let other people tell you what they think of the ten-minute play—what works, what doesn't, and why they're important. Most things will make sense to you; maybe other things won't for now, but it will, in time, and it's all valuable.

Michael Bigelow Dixon
Literary Manager, Actors Theatre of Louisville

Unarguably, few theatre institutions in this country are more responsible for the development of new plays and new playwrights than Actors Theatre of Louisville. Look at a roster of its past seasons dating back to 1976, and what you will see are the most preeminent names not only in the American theatre but throughout the world. There's hardly a living playwright in our day and age who hasn't had at least one play developed through ATL. Doesn't it seem almost predictable, then, that the ten-minute play would find its origins in this fertile playground for play-wrights? In fact, my first memory of any notion of a ten-minute play for the theatre is of the brochure copy of ATL's Humana Festival and its annual National Ten-Minute Play Contest eight years ago.

Almost synonymous with the National Ten-Minute Play Contest is the name of ATL's literary manager, Michael Bigelow Dixon, a gentleman who, along with his staff, reads two thousand-plus manuscripts submitted each year for the contest. I had the pleasure of listening to Dixon respond to a presentation of ten-minute plays as part of the Kennedy Center's National American College Theatre Festival. What those fortunate play-wrights were exposed to was a man who is incredibly bright, articulate, and specific about what makes a successful ten-minute play and what makes interesting, compelling theatre that engages an audience no matter the length.

GG: *Michael, why did ATL institute the National Ten-Minute Play Contest? Where did the idea come from?*

MBD: The National Ten-Minute Play Contest grew out of the National One-Act Play Contest. In early 1978, Jon Jory (the Producing Director of ATL) was looking for a way to build relationships with prominent writers, provide opportunities for emerging writers, find acting roles for our apprentice company, and build special projects into the Humana Festival. So in 1978–79 [in the third annual Festival of New American Plays], we devised two projects for the Humana Festival. First there was an evening titled Holidays [with] ten ten-minute plays by American writers that were inspired by holidays and featured work by playwrights such as John Guare, Marsha Norman, Israel Horovitz, Lanford Wilson, Douglas Turner Ward, and Megan Terry. That project introduced them to ATL and the Humana Festival. What followed from there [1979–80] was the America Project, featuring commissioned ten-minute plays from non-USA playwrights about America and showcased the work of Athol Fugard, Wole Soyinka, Brian Friel, Brian Clark, and Carol Bolt. The ten-minute play built from there and proved useful on four levels: it was good for the playwrights, good for the theatre, offered a fresh exploration of form, and it interested Jon because, like the Humana Festival, it allowed both emerging and established writers to succeed.

GG: *Do you like them [ten-minute plays]?*

MBD: Love the ten-minute play. It's incredibly demanding and offers whatever riches you bring to it. It allows for a feeling of aesthetic eclecticism in an age where people are competing to hear their voices heard. It's a real venue for multicultural, multi-aesthetic concerns.

GG: *Why do you think they are difficult to write?*

MBD: Because they demand complexity and focus, and allow for experimentation and creative riffs. They set high standards for success. Since I read hundreds a year, I'm very aware when the writer fulfills the potential of the story and when the writer's talent fulfills the potential of style and form. Also, since our society is experiencing a glut of stories, the ten-minute play cuts through the exposition and gets right to the conflict and change. You want to see people who are brought to the moment where they are forced to confront something that will change them or not.

GG: *I often hear the concern that focusing on such a short form will rob the writer of his or her ability to write in a longer form. Do you think that's true?*

MBD: The danger seems to be the perception that you'd be creating a David Ives instead of a Tony Kushner. They're both good writers. You could make the argument that the virtues (of writing a ten-minute play) outweigh the problems. It forces you to attend to every line and focus on conflict and character on a moment-to-moment basis. I'd say its virtues are legion because if the building materials aren't compelling, it doesn't matter what length the play is.

GG: *What mistakes do you see writers make when writing the ten-minute play?*

MBD: People try to cover too much ground in the story or narrative instead of concentrating on a moment and they get to the conflict too late [after the first three pages]. Also, they aren't ambitious enough in terms of the spiritual and metaphorical elements—the circumstance never transcends the mundanity of realism. In other words, the play lacks imagination or insight.

GG: *A playwright friend of mine told me about your famous "point, shape, and kick" prescription when writing a ten-minute play. I've never heard it, so . . . would you?*

MBD: "Point, shape, kick" begins with the meaning of the play—that honing and refining of what the author wants to say through the expression of the ten-minute play. What is the *point* of this and how can we maximize it in rehearsal? Because we work hands-on with our playwrights, the playwright's own thinking is part of the revision/refining process. *Shape* implies that there is some action that defines the progress of the play. It may be linear, circular, a jazz motif, anything the playwright creates. Recognizing the shape of the play and fulfilling it is a large part of our process. And the *kick* is something that carries the play: a theatrical value, like surprise or humor, that can carry the audience's attention and energize the dramatic action.

Russ Tutterow
Artistic Director, Chicago Dramatists

Chicago has always been a playwright's town. Visit the city on any day and you'll see a hundred different productions of original work in and around town. Many young and established writers I've known have found their way to Chicago at some point or another in their careers because of the sheer volume of theatres producing new plays. It's an exciting place to be and, for playwrights, made easier to chase that sometimes elusive dream when they're connected to an organization known as Chicago Dramatists. Formed originally in 1979 as a collective of playwrights, the group of artists eventually evolved into a theatre company that nurtures new plays and new playwrights similar to New York City's New Dramatists. In 1986,

Russ Tutterow became the artistic director of the group and has since worked with hundreds of new plays and playwrights.

Chicago Dramatists has a residency program for more experience play-wrights, largely Chicago writers. The Playwrights Network, a resource local playwrights use to develop their work, has a membership of eighty people and anyone can join it at any time. The organization offers a wide variety of playwriting classes and, four times a year, conducts a ten-minute play workshop that culminates in a staged reading for the playwright.

GG: *This is a question I'm throwing at everyone, Russ. Do you like ten-minute plays?*

RT: Love 'em.

GG: *Why?*

RT: It appeals to that area of my brain that has a short attention span. And for us [at Chicago Dramatists] it's attractive: we can work with sev-eral playwrights on one project. As a producer, to read through a whole bunch of short plays lets you get to know a lot more writers, and that's nice. Maybe even more important, though, it's getting a lot more writers on the desk of potential play buyers who are looking to keep an audi-ence. An audience gets to see a great variety of work in a showcase, readings, whatever, and they do great by them. It's always the best audi-ence we have. There are more people involved and they attract more people. You have, even if you do it as a rep company, each actor playing in more than one piece, so it's more fun for the actors and more fun for the audience.

GG: *Some people consider the ten-minute play a lesser form, an "easy workout." What do you think?*

RT: Certainly the newspaper critics that review our productions are not particularly fond of a showcase of multiple short plays. They tend to look upon them as exercises, often comparing one to the other instead of looking at them for what they have to say and how each playwright says it. I don't think that's going to change as long as people consider them as minor. And critics won't ever take them seriously as long as producers don't take them seriously. Some producers will [produce ten-minute plays] to give their company a great project to work on that involves a lot of people, but they leave the people to pretty much produce them on their own, and they look slapdash.

We discovered that, if you were going to do it right, it was very time-consuming and labor-intensive. Our production standards are high, even for an evening of short plays. For many years, we did a showcase of short plays as a major production, but we don't do it anymore and instead devote more time to promote more full-length plays.

GG: *You're around a lot of playwrights. Does it concern you that they're spending energy and time on a short form in a way that might rob them of learning longer forms?*

RT: I don't think they take away from learning to write a longer form, no more so than a writer that works on the same play for twenty years. Television has created the short attention span and playwrights are reacting to that. Is it easier? Yes. Is it less ambitious? Yes. That doesn't necessarily make it bad.

GG: *I know you've seen your share of them, so what do you think makes for a good ten-minute play?*

RT: The most successful ten-minute play, I really believe, has all the same criteria that are in a successful full-length [one]: good storytelling, character, forward motion, structure, and something wonderful. Plays can have big flaws, but as long as there is something wonderful about them, they'll be produced. You don't have time to develop a full story or a full character development—you don't get to develop six characters, but maybe just one. You don't have time for a main plot and two subplots—just one story that plays through. These are the things that elevate a ten-minute play above the level of a revue sketch.

> **Alexa Kelly**
> **Artistic Director and Executive Producer,**
> **Pulse Ensemble Theatre**

Alexa Kelly has been slugging it out in New York City with her Off-Off Broadway theatre company since 1989. Her experience with creating theatre in this city is typical to the New York scene: she makes the very most of a small and somewhat inflexible performance space, operates with limited financial resources, pays for one production with another, competes with countless other theatre companies for an audience, has to nurture an acting company that also functions as a stage crew, and struggles to find dramatic literature that is compelling, interesting to her audience, and easy to produce. But her love for the theatre, limitless energy, and desire to produce thought-provoking, socially challenging theatre enables her to jump past the production obstacles and continue to produce good theatre.

Each month she produces the Opal Series: Open Pulse Arts Lab, wherein original work and, often, ten-minute plays are produced.

GG: *What do you do think of the ten-minute play? Like them? Don't? Love them? Don't?*

AK: I like them. I think they can be a very entertaining and enlightening evening of theatre. If they're good, they can enthrall an audience by leaping about in different places and different times, taking the actors and audience on a global tour of emotional relationships. Inexperienced actors get the experience they need without torturing an audience because they can work within their scope, and whatever happens, it's only going to happen for ten minutes. And actors love them [*Groans*]: they're stars for ten minutes. Young directors benefit greatly because they [the plays] have to be about something dramatic, and be quick about it. The director has to learn to build an emotional life into the play—almost lightning fast—then add more life to it as it goes.

The audience is always surprised how fun the evening can be because I don't think they come with the idea that they are going to be emotionally engaged, and they're surprised when they discover they are. And if they're not, nothing goes on too long for them. If they find they don't like a play, it's only a matter of a few minutes before it's over.

GG: *Any advice you'd give writers?*

AK: I don't always care for one-acts or short plays because they rarely, if ever, feel complete. But if you write a good ten-minute play, it has a point to make and it makes it in a way that feels full. The story may be small, or normal, but the issue is huge—so big that it surprises everyone.

It doesn't wander around (there's no time), trying to find its story or conflict.

And I think the plays that work best in this kind of theatre don't have a beginning, just a middle and an end. They [the playwrights] should plunge into the very middle of a dramatic situation because the beginning can be implicit in the story if it's written well. Let the beginning happen offstage and drop us into a world that is conflicted already. We don't have time to draw the audience in slowly; they have to comprehend what's at stake immediately and care about it from the moment the lights come up.

For my tastes, they should have a little emotional surprise to them. You shouldn't know what they're about—not really, not completely. There should be something very normal about the story, immediately, and then it works well if it has a surprise emotional twist that slowly reveals itself. And that takes you aback when you realize there's a huge scope to what seemed to be a very simple story. And the audience loves—they *love* it— when they think something is about one thing and it turns out it's about something else.

GG: *I think they're hard to produce. I think, mercy, whatta headache. You?*

AK: [*Laughs*] I think they're much easier to produce. Yes, there's double of everything to do. And it takes more organizational ability on the whole struc- ture of the evening to make it work. But we have more playwrights, directors, and actors—more people—to make it work and who bring more people into the theatre because they're involved. You're not playing on any famous name playwright or director, usually, and the actors are the actors you always work with, so that means you can keep everything simple—it has to be about the actors and the story. And if that's the case, you can use six black chairs, two black tables, and two black cubes and create the world of the play with good writing and acting. That's what we do in the Opal Series.

GG: *Just six black chairs, huh? Hmmmm.*

AK: Yes, believe it or not, you can create a world [*Laughs*] despite the lack of furniture.

Laura Margolis
Producing Manager, StageWorks

If Alexa Kelly and Pulse Ensemble Theatre are typical of the perennially struggling Off-Off Broadway theatre company, Laura Margolis and StageWorks are typical of the perennially struggling small professional theatre company outside of a large metropolis. Situated in the city of Hudson just outside of Albany in upstate New York, StageWorks culti- vates an audience from a hundred-mile radius of its performance facility. Laura spends eight months of the year preparing for her four-month sea- son, spanning May to August. For the last four years, StageWorks has produced an annual festival of ten-minute plays, Ten by Ten, thematically centered on one primary color: purple, blue, red, and so on.

GG: *How did that color thing get started?*

LM: Honestly? We thought it was a great way to meet a lot of new writers and to offer something different than just your typical festival of plays. We put together a Ten by Ten committee of theatre and literary professionals, so that they could be charged with reading all the plays and selecting them. When the committee got together, I suggested as the producer that it would more interesting, to my mind, if there was something that tied them together thematically, yet left the writer a lot of room for creativity. We talked about a lot of different things, but the [thematic] use of color seemed to be the most freeing. It was general and yet specific enough to ignite the imagination of the playwright. So far we've done red, green, purple, and black/white.

The first year we presented them as readings in a rough, rough workshop style as a supplement to our mainstage season. They were directed and up on their feet, book in hand. They were overwhelmingly—and almost immediately—popular because it seems that the audience—aside from the writing—enjoyed the search for the color in the course of the play. I know that sounds crazy, but it's true. There's this weird element of "Where is the color?" So in some subliminal or even obvious way, the color ties the evening together and the audience is sort of tricked into taking the ride.

I love the ten-minute play. I feel as a theater artist that we often trap ourselves by what we perceive as limitations. But with any limitation in the theatre, there is immense creative freedom. A whole explosion of creativity is going to open to you when you limit the story of your play to an elevator. But if you put the world of your play in the middle of Grand Central Station, it's less interesting. You've got rules and regulations everywhere in your life, and we all understand that. So in this, you've got ten minutes to explode creatively, and that's just what you should do.

GG: *Writing this book, I'm in that search, that looking-for-an-answer kind of place where I'm trying to figure out what makes an interesting ten-minute play. I'm shy to say a good ten-minute play, 'cause that's so subjective, but I bet you're not shy about it. So what makes a good ten-minute play?*

LM: That's easy. We're looking for what I think everyone else is looking for: a great, compelling story with compelling characters that in ten minutes creates a wonderful theatre experience—it takes us on a journey that deals with circumstances that are identifiable to us emotionally. It's the same stuff of a longer play, only shorter and they jump from the beginning. There's a green light from the moment the play starts that nudges the story to dash out of the starting gate, like, go, go, go. Yeah, I'd say that's one of the key features of a good ten-minute: the green light.

That's for the writer. As producers, we need to put together an evening that is diverse, has a variety of writing styles and approaches to the idea of theatre that stimulates everyone's imagination. Then we get very, um, *dry*, for lack of a better word, about our practicalities of production. For example, we limit the cast size to four because we pull the whole evening off with only six actors, partly for us because it works with the practical realities we face of producing theatre with limited resources, and partly for the audience because it's clear they have fun watching six actors play twenty-five roles. The audience gets to see actors play a huge span of different characters. It's like the old repertory theatre audience; an actor plays a variety of roles throughout the season, but here they see it in one evening.

Producing it requires a whole different head, another way of thinking about your production. You need to have some thought about the transitions and transformation from one play to another, and at the same time, keep the arc of the entire evening in mind. An audience—just like in a full-length play—needs a through line that pulls them through a dramatically compelling evening. This inevitably leads to a discussion of what play to start with, what play to end with, what plays should be in the middle. Do you begin and end with the comedies or the dramas? How do we arrange the evening so that the small group of actors we're using aren't working in plays back to back, exhausting them?

GG: A *lot of work, huh*?

LM: Yeah, but fun work. It's like a jigsaw puzzle. But every year after the production comes down, we've figured out a way to do it more simply for the next year. Each year we're so excited, frankly, that we've figured out how to produce it. It's an achievement. Each year it's all different: the set, the concept, the writers. We create an environment for it all to happen . . .

and it happens, with a lot of work . . . and I guess, a little bit of . . . I don't know, can I say, magic?

B. J. Scott
Artistic Director, Camino Real Playhouse

Like any snotty, East Coast theatre person, I sometimes indulge in those little jabs we all take at the West Coast for its supposed lack of good theatre. The truth of the matter is that extraordinarily vital, important theatre is being done up and down the West Coast. B. J. Scott's small theatre in San Juan Capistrano, California, works hard to engage its local audience with theatre that is both meaningful and entertaining. Camino Real Playhouse has been around for twelve years and has produced eight seasons of theatre. Situated in a Catholic neighborhood, the theatre by necessity has to be family-oriented and conscious about being politically correct—no small task as each year it produces the ShowOff Playwriting Festival, which solicits submissions for ten-minute plays. This year it received 450 submissions.

GG: *So out of that those 450 submissions, how do you decide which to produce?*

BJS: Our main focus is that we find something that will make for an entertaining evening. So we look for something unusual, something different. What we *don't* spend a lot of time reading is the boy meets girl, loses girl, gets girl back kind of play. Or the blind date play, you know, where two people meet in a restaurant. They're so predictable, and I guess we're more drawn to anything that's not [predictable]. Oh, and the sitcom scenario doesn't get very far with us—that one-joke plot thing. Unfortunately, about 90 percent of what we read are those kinds of plays.

GG: *So I take it you've read a few bad ten-minute plays?*

BJS: Yeah, but it's not that the writing is so bad, story to story; it's the lack of an interesting idea in these plays that's so frustrating. When the idea isn't there, quite often there's no character either, or no real story. I guess what I'm really saying is that there has to be a good idea behind the play with characters and a story that support it. And you have to get to it really quickly, kinda like haiku for the theatre. It has to happen on the first page, not the last.

And writers get in their own way, sometimes. They *require* that their plays have a cast of ten. No. I can't do it. There's a comfort level to consider when you have thirty people backstage and your theatre's designed to only have ten. Or a writer will create a character that has to be extremely obese. Well, I don't know that many extremely obese actors, so right away I'm limited. Which doesn't mean you shouldn't write the play you want to write, but you do have to remember that I have to produce it. And yes, we've got plenty of actors around, but I don't always know if I can find three black actors and two Asian actresses in order to produce your play. I'll always try, but I also have to remember who I have to play with. Sometimes it all comes down to just that: who do I know that can play these characters? I'm one to keep it as simple as possible.

GG: *Actors really seem to like to work on ten-minute plays. Is that your experience?*

BJS: Absolutely, it's attractive to a lot of professional actors because it's not a huge commitment. I know actors who won't audition for a regular play, but will audition for the ten-minute play festival because you rehearse it eight times and you're up. You can bank on a short time period and you don't have to learn a jillion lines. Actually, it's very time-efficient for each of the creative components because there's not all of the stuff that goes into a full production—the long technical rehearsals, changing costumes three or four times because you're changing seasons three or four times. With a ten-minute play, it's more immediate, it's more of the moment.

GG: *And your audiences like them?*

BJS: The audiences love them. Don't get me wrong, they don't appeal to everyone, but most people who see them like them. And the press eats it up. It's giving new writers a forum because these are playwrights that might not be heard otherwise. And it's all so varied. You can watch one that you really hate and know you're not trapped in the theatre because in ten minutes it'll all be over. That's not so bad.

Gregg Henry
Artistic Director, The John F. Kennedy Center's
American College Theatre Festival

Gregg recently came into his position of artistic director for the Kennedy Center's American College Theatre Festival (KC/ACTF). Having served in his own region of the country (the Midwest) for several years as its regional chair for KC/ACTF, Gregg was responsible for programming at the regional festival, where hundreds of student actors, directors, playwrights, and designers gathered to celebrate the college theatre of that region. Now, in his new position, not only does he do the same for the national festival held each year in Washington, D.C., but he's responsible for the almost-bursting-at-the-seams opportunities afforded student playwrights as part of the Kennedy Center's educational mission. One such opportunity was the inauguration and development of a student National Ten-Minute Play Festival that's heading into its fourth year.

GG: *The Kennedy Center's American College Theatre Festival took a big step three years ago by instituting a National Ten-Minute Play Festival. Why do you think they got behind it?*

GH: I can't speculate why it moved [from the regions] to Washington [and the National Festival] so fast. I think it would be safe to say that what we saw happening at the regional level was an incredible opportunity for playwrights to write in a difficult but manageable form and, long story short, see their work performed at a festival of new works. The other benefit, of course, was the collaborative opportunities. I think what we came to understand was we had a project where strangers—actors, playwrights, and directors—would be thrown together and by the end of *x* period, they would bond and make something happen. That's the ACTF phenomena when we're doing it right: building and sharing things together in a brief but intense period. So for us, it really serves two functions: it furthers the unspoken mission in that it introduces young artists to one another and it provides young artists with some pretty essential theatre tools.

GG: *I know you have some . . . difficulties . . . with the whole notion of a ten-minute play. Want to share?*

GH: Reservations . . . hmmmm. What are they? Well, first is form: I think when they're done well, and right, they're a terrific tool or exercise in having the playwright understand [dramatic] structure. *Bang*, lay out the facts, *crash*, get the complications in there and work to resolve the problem, *thwak*, end. The whole thing should be this complete, tight theatre experience. But that's not what happens a lot of the time. What I see are *not* ten-minute plays; they're interesting scenes. Last year, I was a respondent to a bill of ten-minute plays, and I heard myself keep saying, "This is not a ten-minute *play*, because I want to know more about this person and more about what it's about," because what *was there* felt so incomplete. I kept seeing character studies that were charming, but incomplete plays.

Another worry is that it's too easy to fall into a "this is quick and easy" kind of mentality, and then what you get are a lot of revues or Saturday Night Live sketches. The ten-minute restriction plucks at the attention span—which we know is about a steady seven minutes in the entertainment field. That's what television commercials have done for us. And I also worry that some think, "I can do this," but they don't take the next step of learning a fuller form.

I think ten-minute plays teach structure, and that's a good thing, but they come with their share of bad-writer things. I'm not saying let's adhere to [Aristotle's] *Poetics*, but longer forms give the playwright time to lay out the givens, a little more leisure time to lay out the exposition and that crack of inciting incident. Too often [with a ten-minute play], somebody is getting rewarded for writing a sketch, which might be the right length but is not a play.

GG: *You've long been an actor, theatre director, administrator, and acting teacher. Are there problems that you see with ten-minute plays that tend to trip up the actor? Or better yet, what actor problems inevitably reveal themselves when an actor is working on a ten-minute play?*

GH: Just as I think it is a great tool for a writer, particularly when it comes to establishing character quickly and getting the necessary emotional information across to the audience efficiently, I think it's a great tool for the actor because [he or she has] to do the exact same thing. I have always been a cheerleader for big, strong, bold choices, and a ten-minute play allows the actors just that. They don't have the luxury of time. You walk on stage and something has to be emanating out of every pore of your person. [Jon] Jory [of the Actors Theatre of Louisville] says the play starts with a lightning bolt; both actors and directors need to learn that. How do you grab, and how do you hold?

I always get a case of blue balls when I work on a scene with student actors because I always find myself saying, "oh, do you know what comes next," or "do you know what came before it," because there's always something before or after a scene in a longer play. But I found myself assigning and recommending ten-minute plays in directing class because if it's a good ten-minute play, there's a sense of satisfaction because we have seen it all—you can find the mechanism of the whole thing.

GG: *Think they'll be around for a while? Or is it all just a passing fancy?*

GH: I think they'll be around for a long while. I do. I think, too, the more I read the collections, the more I see people understand now what they can do, what they can be, and what they can accomplish. More and more playwrights seem to have a Jory lightning bolt after lightning bolt and produce these beautiful poetic jewels. And if the writer does his job, it's whole, and satisfying. But I still need my *Arcadias* that take their time, make me laugh and cry in a full evening. I still like myself to be engaged over a longer period of time.

> ### Judith Royer
> ### Playwrights Program, Association for Theatre in Higher Education, and Regional Chair, New Plays Program, The Kennedy Center's American College Theatre Festival

Interviewing Judith, I have a quadruple resource: not only is she a freelance director who's worked with countless playwrights developing their plays through production, but she's also a professor of acting and directing at Loyola Marymount University in Los Angeles. In addition, she has served for years in a leadership position in the Playwrights Program of the Association for Theatre in Higher Education, a service organization that brings academics-artists together by discipline. And as if that didn't provide her enough new plays to work on, she has been the West Coast's regional chair for the New Plays Program of the Kennedy Center's American College Theatre Festival, which brings together student playwrights. Here is a woman with extraordinary experience with new plays written by playwrights that span all ages, cultural backgrounds, varieties of education, and professional affiliations. And lucky for all of us, Judith has fostered the development of the ten-minute play not only in her region of the country but throughout the United States through her affiliation with the Kennedy Center.

GG: *You've worked with so many different kinds of playwrights from so many different backgrounds and abilities. And I know I've been witness to your witnessing of hundreds of ten-minute plays. Is there any one universal truth that resonates in you about the whole of it?*

JR: We all seem to underestimate what a difficult form it is and forget that we can't treat it like a sketch. It's a much more difficult form because it has to have everything a long play has with the same clarity of action. I see a lot of character studies that try to be ten-minute plays, and they're interesting, but they're little more than character sketches for a longer play.

The trick is to find an action line that pays off in some meaningful way. And I know how hard that is, for young writers and old. But I also know that we foster a lot of ten-minute plays that haven't hit the mark yet because we often want to foster the playwright, just not necessarily the play. The ten-minute play seems to be an ideal form to encourage and support the less experienced writer because it's challenging, but manageable.

GG: *So they're a good thing for writers?*

JR: For the experience of learning their craft, yes. But they need to be kicked beyond that. I see a lot of MFA writing programs using the form to teach, and that's great. But in the professional theatre, we're ending up with submissions that are just collections of ten-minute plays. I see plenty of writers who can handle the ten-minute form but can't write a longer play; they can't sustain a multifaceted story and instead just write a lot of ambiance and dialogue.

As an acting teacher, they're wonderful for young actors because they're not taking cuttings from longer plays that you're not sure they fully understand anyway. Student actors can handle the form if it's well written and brings together all the good elements of drama. And for young directing students, it's a perfect teaching tool because, again, it's manageable. As a director myself, it's more of an exercise than anything else. You're literally hitting that action line and going with it, and that's it. You just clarify that action line. There's never much rehearsal time, so you let your actors take their own leads and let them go.

GG: *Okay, so I'm gonna skip over the "do you like them" kind of questions, because frankly it seems that everybody likes them. Here's my question to you: what don't you like about them?*

JR: [*Laughs*] The fact that you don't see many good ones.

GG: *Why do you think?*

JR: Some writers are literally only interested in how clever they can turn the ending or the initial assumption: God and the Devil caught in an elevator, going up and down between Heaven and Hell. That's the device. Somehow there has to be something that will grab you on a level that isn't just clever, and that can still go somewhere in ten minutes.

For the writer, there is no time to develop much character; subtlety and complexity is hard to pull off in ten minutes but is so needed. And when it is written with subtlety and complexity, I don't know that directors and actors can pull it off because there's usually never much time to rehearse them. Everyone underestimates the process, and it becomes all about getting it up. And the really good ten-minute plays need time. I've spent more time on a four-minute piece than a twenty-minute piece because with less material, there's more to bring to life. And, because it's really, really short, you either hit the first beat, or you never get there. Either you jump on the roller coaster or not.

GG: *What's your biggest headache when you go about producing a bill of ten-minute plays, even if it's for just a sit-down reading?*

JR: Personnel. Specifically directors. No matter how well you think you've selected, how many resumes you've looked at, how many people you've talked to, I've found if there's a consistent problem in production, it's usually with a director, or more specifically, a director's ego. Let's face it: a lot of people don't know how to work with this format or with new, original work and playwrights. There's so little time—literally—in both the production and the play, and I see a lot of directors that don't know how to get out of the way of the material because their own egos are involved. They burden the plays with too much attention. They see it as they've only got ten minutes to make their mark, and they're so afraid that if they haven't staged it brilliantly, it reflects on them.

They should clarify the story with the writer and actors and just make sure the story's being told. And that's a very special skill. A full-length play doesn't afford them the time to focus so intensely and almost unrelentingly on its presentation. And when they do that with a ten-minute play, you hear about hours and hours of rehearsal scheduled because they [the directors] are looking a this little moment and that little moment, and the plays suddenly become double their actual length.

GG: *Any last thoughts?*

JR: It's a consummate art, when you think about it.

CHAPTER

Drying Out Your Mouth

My God . . . now what? —Michel Wallerstein, playwright, on finishing a ten-minute play

YOU'RE FINISHED. DONE. YOU'VE READ IT TEN TIMES SINCE WRITING "Lights fade," reread it again with emotions, without emotions, with accents, without the accents, laughed at your own jokes, and assured yourself that Uncle Donnie *could not, would not*, without a shadow of a doubt, fall asleep during this play. You've saved the computer file on eight different disks and made five paper copies: one you put in the freezer in case the apartment catches fire, one you mailed to yourself for copyright purposes, one you gave to your best friend to read 'cause she'll love it, one you gave to your teacher 'cause he'll hate it and you need that punishment to keep you writing well, and one you've kept on your desk as a symbol of "See, I can finish something."

Now what?

Big question. Big ol' empty, frustrating, confounding question, "Because who's really going to produce a ten-minute play anyway?" you think. Your mouth instantly dries out. Is it anxiety because you don't know what to do or where to send your play, or is it the anticipation of licking stamps for the self-addressed stamped envelope? Here's the good news: that dry mouth syndrome is now easily remedied.

First, most theatres don't want you to send an SASE because they won't/can't/don't want to return your play—it's too much of an administrative headache for the volume of work they receive. Second, there are scores of places that are looking for short plays, monologue plays, and ten-minute plays. Every day a new theatre discovers the benefits of producing an evening of ten-minute plays. Every day colleges and universities, drama clubs and small groups of actors all stumble upon the joy of creating a night of different voices with intriguing viewpoints on issues that concern their audience. You shouldn't have trouble finding a place to send your ten-minute play, but you might have trouble getting someone them to read it if you don't follow a few simple suggestions and acknowledge a few realities:

1. There are too many of us (playwrights) and too few of them (theatres who routinely produce new original work). Your first job, then, is to make your work known in such a way as to invite not only the submission of your current play but any other work you might have. This starts with taking the time to research where and how to submit your play and then *believing* and honoring your research.

   If you read the *Dramatists Guild Sourcebook*, the Theatre Communications Group *Dramatists Sourcebook* (the best listing of soliciting theatres I know of), or *The Playwright's Companion*, and the description in the submission process notes that the theatre is not looking for kitchen realism, believe it. If the description says that you should submit from January to May, believe it. If the description says that it'll take six months for a response, believe it (then add two additional months). If the description says "plays for women by women," believe it. If the description requests a synopsis, don't try to forget that you read that and hope they won't notice it's missing from your package. If the solicitation description says that the company is looking for plays with six characters or under, why would you send a play with nine? Do you think they won't see the other three? Or do you think that they'll be so taken with your play that the three additional characters won't matter? Believe it—they want six or under! Every artistic director and literary manager that I've had the pleasure of doing business with remarks consistently that writers either don't read, don't believe, or don't honor their submission descriptions.

2. Submit what the theatre asks for, nothing more, nothing less, and make it *easy* for them. This is particularly true when there's a page limit or a character limit. Remember, you're trying to sell them something on

their time. So if a theatre is asking for play that's no more than ten pages and has four characters or fewer, don't waste your time or theirs if your play doesn't match that description.

What's included in a submission package is a letter of introduction followed by either a resume, a synopsis, and/or the full text. This means you have to learn to write a business letter of introduction that (a) isn't cute, (b) doesn't ramble, (c) isn't bitter, (d) isn't so long that they might as well have read the play, but (e) is short, direct, and acknowledges their particular interests and why your play is suitable for their consideration.

This introductory letter is their first exposure to your writing. Don't blow it off because it's only a letter. It should simply state that you're responding to their solicitation for ten-minute plays in blah-blah-blah magazine or journal and that you're enclosing a copy of your play (cite the title). Then briefly describe the story of the play using every creative writing skill you've ever been taught. Seduce the reader into wanting to read the play, but keep it short. Something to avoid in your letter: "This is an uproarious comedy," or "This is a heartbreaking account of . . ." Let someone else be the judge. If you have any questions about your description, give it to somebody who knows your play and ask for a fair assessment. You didn't write your play without feedback, why chance the description?

3. A full-text submission should be either stapled or hole-punched and bradded or secured in a thin folder. Never use paper clips; they fall off. And don't waste your money on a sturdy binder. They take up too much room. Above all else, make sure your page numbers are visibly printed.

The first page of your manuscript is a cover page with your name, address, phone number, and e-mail address. The next page contains a character breakdown that specifies each character's name, age, and sex and a brief description of who he or she is. The text begins on the next page after that. And just so we're all clear about this: the first page of your play with action and dialogue is page 1, not the cover page or character breakdown.

I've seen so many plays ignored, dismissed, and rejected because the playwright didn't follow the simple rule of submission. Don't do that to yourself. Celebrate what you've written and try to share it with the rest of the world.

The following places are looking specifically for ten-minute plays. If there are no specific guidelines mentioned, write or call the theatre before submitting your play.

> Actors Theatre of Louisville
> National Ten-Minute Play Contest
> 316 West Main Street
> Louisville, KY 40202–4218
>
> Website: www.actorstheatre.org/information/
> contest/javelina.html
>
> *Deadline: December 1*

Each playwright may submit only one script. No scripts will be returned—save postage. No SASE required. Entries will be acknowledged by postcard in January. All playwrights will be notified when or before the winner is announced in the fall. Each script must be no more than ten pages long. Previously submitted plays, plays that have received an Equity production, musicals, children's shows, and any unsolicited longer one-act or full-length plays will not be accepted and will be returned. Each manuscript must be typed and individually bound or stapled. Title page must include name, address, and phone number. The volume of scripts submitted hampers ATL's ability to comment individually on each work, so we do not offer criticism.

> The Actors Theater
> David Tulli, Associate Artistic Director
> Box 5858
> Providence, RI 02903

Plays 10 to 30 minutes long that depict "non-stereotypical men" exploring feelings about relationships, sex, self-image, and violence.

> Camino Real Playhouse
> ShowOff Playwriting Festival, Tom Scott, Director
> S.O.CCT. Playwriting Contest
> 31776 El Camino Real

San Juan Capistrano, CA 92675
(949) 248-0808

Send standard paper, stapled. Scripts will not be returned. Include contact information on script; all submissions acknowledged. Prefer ten-minute plays unpublished; single scene; any subject matter; musicals and plays for children considered.

Chicago Dramatists
1005 W. Chicago Ave.
Chicago, IL 60622
(312) 633-0630

Website: www.centerstage.net/chicago/theatre/theatres/
chicago-dramatists.html

Unsolicited scripts not accepted for regular season. Unsolicited scripts for 10-Minute Workshop must be preceded by a phone call requesting guidelines. **Special programs**: quarterly ten-minute play workshop.

City Playhouse
Short Play Festival
LACC Theatre Academy
855 N. Vernon Ave.
Los Angeles, CA 90029
(213) 953-4336

Plays 10 to 15 minutes long; must be typed and bound; scripts will not be returned.

City Theatre
PO Box 248268
Coral Gables, FL 33124
(305) 204-3605

Plays should be ten minutes or less; limit two scripts. Must be typed, bound, and include SASE for return. Multicultural acting company; bilingual plays considered.

CollaborAction Theatre Company
1945 West Henderson
Chicago, IL 60657–2016
Attn: Submissions

Deadline: December 15

Special interests: contemporary mini-plays with strong focus on narrative
and character. Submissions must perform under ten minutes.

Curtain Time Players
Attn: Robert Redd, Artistic Director
PO Box 256
Ada, MI 49301
(616) 676-1583

Interested in seniors' issues, family problems, intergenerational issues;
comic if possible.

Emerging Artists Theatre Company
518 Ninth Avenue, Suite 2
New York, NY 10018
Attn: Paul Adams
(212) 627-5792

Website: www.eatheatre.org

One-acts twenty pages or less.

E.S.T. In Aspen, HBO Comedy Arts Festival
Risa Bramon Garcia & Debra Stricklin,
Executive Producers
2049 Century Park East, 42d Floor
Los Angeles, CA 90067
(310) 201-9575

Send three copies of each play. Limit three plays. New one-act comedies,
10 to 40 minutes long.

Plays the Thing Productions
PO Box 16449
San Diego, CA 92176

Deadline: August 31

No previous Equity productions. $100 first prize, $75 second prize, $50 third prize; fifteen performances.

Pulse Ensemble Theatre
Open Pulse Arts Lab
432 W. 42d Street
New York, NY 10036
(212) 695-1596

Monthly productions of short plays, monologues, mono-dramas, one-acts in the OPAL (Open Pulse Arts Lab) Series. Send inquiries about the OPAL writers workshop to the above address.

Sub-Orbit Blowout Theatre Co.
Attn: Alex Exum
70 South Main Street, Suite 401
Norwalk, CT 06854

Info: exum@onebox.com

Deadline: August 20

SUNY/Brockport, Department of Theatre
Attn: Richard St. George
Chairman, Department of Theatre
350 New Campus Drive
SUNY College at Brockport
Brockport, NY 14420

Deadline: September 30

Each script bound in a secure folder. Include name, address, telephone number on title page. Not Equity produced.

Theatre Oxford
Ten Minute Play Contest
PO Box 1321
Oxford, MS 38665

Deadline: February 1

Send SASE for guidelines.

The Kennedy Center's American College Theatre Festival
(address varies depending on your region of the country)

There is a ten-minute (seven to ten pages, twelve-point font) limit for each play. Plays that arrive at the Kennedy Center will be cut if their running time is longer than ten minutes. The ten-minute play competition is limited to students enrolled in a college or university during the festival year.

Eligibility for entering a ten-minute play in the national showcase is based on whether the playwright's school has entered a participating or associate level entry in KC/ACTF during the festival year. Plays from schools that do not have a participating or associate entry will submit a $20 fee for each ten-minute play, payable to the region.

The national winning ten-minute play will be selected prior to the national festival and will be based on readings of the eligible finalist scripts. The Kennedy Center's American College Theater Festival is pleased to announce the third annual Ten-Minute Play Festival at the KC/ACTF National Festival. A first-place award of $1,000 will be given to the playwright selected from the national festival finalists. Selection of the national winner is based on a reading of the eight finalists' plays by the national selection team. For more information on entering a ten-minute play, contact the New Plays Program chair in your region of the country. If you're unfamiliar with who this person is, visit the KC/ACTF website <http://kennedy-center.org/education/actf>.

West Coast Ten-Minute Play Contest and Festival
Jill Forbath Roden, Artistic Director
PO Box 18438
Irvine, CA 92623–8438
(949) 552-6256

7

CHAPTER

Body Parts

[When you asked me to write a play for this book] it crossed my mind that I had a good reason to call my agent with this happy news of a publication (gotta keep that connection lively). Then it occurred to me that he really wouldn't give a damn. So I told my mother-in-law, who's the only person who seems genuinely impressed by my doings. She said: "But, why don't you write a real play?" —Wendy Yondorf, playwright

TRYING TO DECIDE HOW TO SHARE EXAMPLES OF TEN-MINUTE plays with you has been a big, splittin' headache. Do I give you what I think are five of the best plays I can find? Do I show you plays that are good but have all kinds of structural problems so that we can have a hot discussion of their strengths and weaknesses? Do I compare one with the other, or make no comparisons at all and let you draw the your own conclusions? Should I share a play with you that's too early in its development to really be appreciated for the germ of the idea that it is?

What stumped me for the longest time was that I can't be sitting across a table from you, seeing a quizzical look on your face and helping you decipher what you may or may not understand. I can't be there to hear you laugh or throw this book down when you get confused or even bored with one of the plays. And I can't give you a writing aesthetic that contends that "this is good, and this isn't" without understanding more of your own sensibility. So what I'm going to do is ask you questions—lots of questions—about five plays that were all written around the same thematic idea by wildly different playwrights.

I asked five writers, different in style, taste, and sensibilities, to engage themselves to write a ten-minute play from one simple idea: let a body part inspire the writing. I don't know about you, but my body is something that I'm completely in conflict with every day of my life. One day I hate it, the next day I'm showing it off in too-tight jeans and a too-small T-shirt. I watch it age, muscle up, lose muscle, get fat, get thin, grow hair, lose hair, grow bumps, and make dents. And no matter what I do to it, how I treat it, gawk at it, or ignore it, it's still there when I wake up in the morning. So I thought giving the writers this assignment was sure to produce, at the very least, some inherent dramatic tension even if the inspiration came from a place of admiration.

I chose the five playwrights for this book because they've all written a lot of ten-minute plays and seen many of their own produced. And for the most part, I think they're writers who enjoy the challenge of writing the ten-minute play because it's quick in relation to other work they might do as playwrights (all five writers were working on longer plays when asked to write for this book). Said playwright Gary Sunshine, "You know you're not going to be holding the audience hostage for more than ten minutes; if you take big risks and you lose the audience, or fail to engage them, no one's going to punish you too severely for ten minutes of confusion or aggravation." Wendy Yondorf has a different kind of comfort with the ten-minute play: "In my experience with this format, I've found an event and a vision sort of burble up in my mind and I know the beginning, middle, and end, which is never the case when I'm writing a full-length play." Tish Benson simply said, ". . . for me, it was a pleasure to nail down something in my life that wasn't girth-heavy."

And were they satisfied with their own results? Michel Wallerstein echoed a sentiment all five writers expressed at one point or another when he admitted, "I keep asking myself: is this interesting? If I'm the audience, do I care who these people are and what happens to them? And because I'm an insecure mess, I usually don't get the answers until I finish writing whatever I'm working on and give it to someone I trust . . ." David Crespy answered this question with a more philosophical view of all kinds of dramatic writing for the theatre: "I just think it's part of the job of the dramatist to write from the heart and put oneself at risk in the writing of a play. If a play doesn't cost you something to write, then maybe it's not really worth the effort . . . Bottom line, it has cost me something to write this play, to reveal myself as a human being, and I think that's part of your job as a writer. We're not paid to write things anyone can write. We owe our audiences a play that is terrifying for us to write, that forces us to take risks . . ."

Read the work, take notes, and look at the author's comments and questions that follow each play. I guarantee you'll learn something.

A TAIL
by Gary Sunshine

SHERRI, *a nerdy woman in her 20s, wearing a tam, sits on a tantalizingly comfortable upholstered chair at a suburban Starbucks, knitting. Next to her is a wooden, empty chair and a small coffee table. PAULINE, in her 30s dressed like she's trying to look chic but just can't cut it, enters, sees the line is too long, spots SHERRI's chair, crosses to it, hovers, then finally says:*

PAULINE: Warm.

SHERRI: Yes.

PAULINE: Cozy.

SHERRI: Yes.

PAULINE: Crowded . . . but cozy.

SHERRI: Yes.

Pause.

PAULINE: You look around, you scan the place, you see wood, hard wood, not splintery, but wood all the same, wood that will abrade your coccyx if you're not blessed with a well-padded coccyx, although natural padding is both a blessing and a curse, padding protects but it alienates and the greatest curse is to be alone, contemplating one's coccyx, my, what a luscious chair you have.

Pause. PAULINE starts to sit in the empty chair.

SHERRI: My friend's coming.

PAULINE: You have a friend?

SHERRI: Yes. She's my friend.

PAULINE: She. Does she have a well-padded coccyx?

SHERRI: That's not something we talk about.

PAULINE: So you're not intimate?

SHERRI: I don't know how much she weighs.

PAULINE: Weight indicates the amount of pressure applied to your coccyx every time you sit upon an awful wooden chair. There are so many awful wooden chairs in the world, so few that give comfort. Does she have a name?

Pause.

SHERRI: She has a name.

PAULINE: It isn't Jacinda, is it?

SHERRI: It isn't Jacinda.

PAULINE: OK. (*Pause*) Is her name Rain? Or Firestorm? Something ecofriendly?

Silence.

PAULINE (*Cont.*): What time is she coming?

SHERRI: Excuse me?

PAULINE: You said a friend would join you. I'd like to know when you're expecting her. That's all. What time? That's all.

SHERRI: Eleven.

PAULINE: It's past eleven. Twelve past eleven.

SHERRI: She's late.

PAULINE: She's made other arrangements.

SHERRI: Do you know my friend?

PAULINE: It's a rejection but a minor one.

SHERRI: She'll be here.

PAULINE: This table gets an awful lot of sun.

SHERRI: Yes.

PAULINE: You can't hide from the sun.

SHERRI: I'm not hiding.

PAULINE: No, you're beyond that. You're disappearing.

SHERRI: I must be someone else to you.

PAULINE: I feel as though we know each other.

SHERRI: We've never met. Not even now.

PAULINE: You're the one who admires Jacinda and Rain from afar. As you do all the in-crowd. An onlooker, that's who I'm talking to. You think you live in a silent sob—

SHERRI: —I never cry—

PAULINE: —Frankly, desperation has a noise to it, high-pitched but it exists, it can make your ears bleed. But there's great news, Koko, I'll call you Koko, Koko with kays, not cees. Anyone with a tail can have a conversation, Koko. A mule can say "Yes," or "That's hilarious!"

SHERRI: I don't have a tail.

PAULINE: We used to have tails. I believe the coccyx is all we have left to remind us of our carefree days in the wild. Have you ever wondered what it would be like to have a tail? Can I sit here? Please. I'd like to sit here and talk about tails. Or not.

Silence. PAULINE *sits.* SHERRI *stands.* PAULINE *stands.* SHERRI *sits.* PAULINE *sits.*

PAULINE (*Cont.*): Our two chairs are Darwinian endpoints, all of evolution flows between us. I sit at the rather uncomfortable beginning of time, you at the heavenly end. In that darling chair. Does your friend regularly stand you up?

SHERRI: No one has stood me up. She had a date last night. She's probably tired. She probably got up late. Maybe she went to the gym. And then I bet she went to the beauty parlor. Then she probably snuck in a facial, just to get herself going. Maybe she scheduled an emergency massage, she has this guy come to her apartment, he's a secular monk, and he puts on some soothing music . . .

PAULINE: I was like you once. On the sidelines. Very quiet. Wanting a real friend more than anything in the world.

SHERRI: A real friend.

PAULINE (*Cont.*): How did I evolve? I'd make a call. I have a yellow phone shaped like a banana. I'd dial up Rosie O'Donnell, or Kirstie Alley, or Cicely Tyson—

SHERRI: —You have famous friends?

PAULINE: No. But only because they refused to return my calls. At first I thought it was my voice, it was very plain, very uninflected. I'm from a flat place, originally, it lacks elevation, it's the topographical equivalent of your hair. So I'd gussy up my delivery a bit. Started to speak with a bit of a brogue. That didn't work.

SHERRI: Maybe you needed to show them you were a person of varied interests. I knit. And I do hook rugs. I also collect zippers.

PAULINE: . . . Anyway, I switched to a drawl, hoping it would impart a certain cordiality, a warmth. But I got nowhere.

SHERRI: Some connections aren't meant to connect.

PAULINE: How many times have you said *that* to yourself alone in the dark?

Pause. SHERRI *gathers up her belongings and looks out at the room for a new place to sit.* PAULINE *starts to creep into* SHERRI's *chair.* SHERRI *spots her and* PAULINE *quickly retreats.*

PAULINE (*Covering*): Yes, so, you've got a little *wanderlust*? Ready to venture out in search of your fortune?

SHERRI: It's just so packed.

PAULINE: Do you know anyone here?

SHERRI: They're all strangers.

PAULINE: I was a stranger. Look how far we've come.

SHERRI: You don't even know my name.

PAULINE: But I know so much about you. You're a bright young woman with a fondness for tams and yarn and unattainable friendships and comfortable chairs.

SHERRI: That doesn't begin to scratch my surface.

PAULINE: Trade chairs with me and I'll plunge your depths.

SHERRI: I can't.

PAULINE: On principle?

SHERRI: Yes.

PAULINE: After all we've meant to each other?

SHERRI: We mean nothing to each other.

PAULINE: But we will. In the long run. You like what I have to say. I like the texture of your chair. That sort of bond resonates through the ages.

SHERRI (*Suddenly screaming*): THIS CHAIR IS MINE!!! (*Pause. Barely audible*) This chair is mine . . .

PAULINE: The damage is done.

SHERRI: I'm sorry.

PAULINE: Words can't hurt but the tone, the tone sliced my heart.

SHERRI: I don't know what came over me.

PAULINE: Koko, darling, I've opened my soul to you. That's the rarest, most valiant of acts, and how do you repay me? Eons of rage and brutality concentrated into one, full-throated thunderbolt—

SHERRI: —They take things from me. At work. We wear aprons so we won't get the ink on us from the photocopiers. They took my apron. They took my lunch, deviled ham and a blonde brownie. They took my Knitter's World calendar out of my locker, as if they even give a fish about handcrafts. They even took my Soft Soap, it was the chamomile kind, very hard to find consistently. And I was tired of slithering home. I've been slithering home all of my life. So I took action, finally. I went to this clinic down near the water. This man, his name was Mr. Lawson, he told me things about standing up for my rights. He said only animals take what doesn't belong to them. He said the world has become a very mean place and the only way to hold onto things is to call upon the animal within.

PAULINE: I like that. What's yours?

SHERRI: Mr. Lawson says I can't ever reveal that, not even to him.

The animal within has to remain in hiding. You can call him out only in times of great need.

PAULINE: Passionate need.

SHERRI: Yes.

PAULINE: Did I trigger your passion? Or was it strictly the chair?

SHERRI: I don't have total control over my powers yet.

PAULINE: It was me. We did connect. We did know each other. For a moment. Once.

SHERRI *looks away, very embarrassed. She grabs her knitting needles and begins to knit with increasing passion, struggling not to look at* PAULINE.

Hot red light suddenly floods the table.

PAULINE: I have a coccyx. Three moveable bones that will eventually fuse into a beak but once, once there was a tail.

SHERRI: I had a tail.

PAULINE: My tail made decisions.

SHERRI: Mine was furry.

PAULINE: It told me which way to go, it got me places.

SHERRI: It brushed away the tall grasses and made the river part.

PAULINE: It spoke for me. A thud against the jungle dirt, a slice through the hot angry air.

SHERRI: I hung from my tail in the hot angry air.

PAULINE: There were no words.

SHERRI: No frappucinos.

PAULINE: No stupid bullshit just a tail and a body and a sky made of green and red feathers and there was a pack of beasts and I was a member of that pack—

SHERRI: —Not off on the sidelines—

PAULINE: —We wandered together—

SHERRI: —We squawked and flew through the vines—

PAULINE: —And there were no unreturned phone calls no unanswered personal ads no sitting alone in the back row of the movie house—

SHERRI: In the wild we linked our tails together—

PAULINE: —In the wild we were never alone—

SHERRI: —When we had tails.

PAULINE: When we had tails.

Lights return to normal. SHERRI scrambles away from PAULINE. Long pause.

SHERRI: I don't think she's coming. My friend.

PAULINE: No.

SHERRI: She's very busy. My friend. This happens.

PAULINE: I could be your friend.

SHERRI: If I gave you my chair?

PAULINE: A simple gesture can spark years of commitment.

SHERRI: I'll give you the chair and you'll never speak to me again.

PAULINE: Or we could wind up spending our Saturday nights in my backyard, roasting hot dogs, drinking gin and tonics and hanging upside down from my apple tree. Making a helluva lot of noise.

Pause. SHERRI gathers up her things, rises, and begins to exit.

PAULINE quickly sits herself down in SHERRI's chair and luxuriates. SHERRI watches this from afar. She returns to the table. She reaches into her bag and pulls out a tubular creation she has knitted. She places it on the table and leaves.

Silence.

Tentatively, PAULINE reaches for the knitted piece, unfurls it, rises, and affixes it to the back of her slacks, so that it hangs like a tail. She lifts the end of it, and looks toward the door, as the lights fade to black.

END OF PLAY

GARY SUNSHINE ON A TAIL

When I thought about writing [from an inspiration of] body parts, I figured I should pick one that spoke to me. My body only speaks to me when it's in need of medical attention. My second choice was my esophagus, because that particular organ and I have had such a nasty relationship as of late, but I couldn't imagine my way into ten minutes inside someone else's esophagus. So I chose the coccyx. I actually got intrigued by a situation I had observed, and wanted to make it into a play, and it involved people sitting down, or wanting to sit down. Other body parts involved in sitting provided too inelegant a place to start.

As always, I really didn't know what I was going to write when I sat down. I had some elements. Coccyx. Starbucks. Two great chairs. A person sitting in a chair, another one approaching her, wanting something very badly, needing to oust the sitting person in order to get what she wanted. I wasn't sure if there were a third character involved, if this were a triangle. I didn't quite know what the relationship between these people was—Were they total strangers? Lovers? And I started hearing a bit of a jungle beat, flashes of the Discovery Channel. I just gave myself over to it and figured I'd wind up somewhere in ten pages. I gave it to my partner, who is forced to read everything I write, because I am a tyrant, and all writers need someone to bear the brunt of their tyrannical narcissism. He thought I had made an interesting if confusing, muddled start. He gave me a few suggestions—as always his suggestions forced me back to my original impulses; that's the greatest gift he gives to me as a reader. I went back in, got clearer, made firmer decisions, and finished it off.

I wrote about Starbucks. Starbucks on Sheridan Square has become my office; I get the Zen tea and a dry bagel and poof, I'm liberated from the dark corners of my apartment. The area in *my* Starbucks where the play takes place is actually drenched in sunlight—it's the only seat near a window. It's sort of like a little stage, this table by the window. It's the first image you get of the place from the street. Also, because these are the best seats in this location, it feels as though there's a lot of focus directed toward whomever happens to land this particular setup. If you're going to sit in great chairs, you've got a responsibility to your fellow frappuchino drinkers to be interesting and entertaining. At first, I thought I wanted to write about that kind of responsibility—the pressure to be an interesting person. But as I wrote on, I realized I really wanted to talk about the covetousness that reveals itself all around us, all the time, especially in capitalist culture. As soon as one person sees another with something he or she wants, a battle will ensue at some level. And underneath this constant drive to acquire—to take from others—is a very strange, dualistic set of impulses—to destroy the person who has what you want, and to connect, to avoid being alone, to create connection at all costs. I love this kind conflict, because it is at once so heartbreaking, yet hopeful. We kill each other but we'd really rather go off and drink martinis together, I'd like to think.

READER QUESTIONS

1. We've talked about how each character in your ten-minute play should want something, *need* something, and either get what he or she wants or not get it. What do Sherri and Pauline need in A *Tail*? What obstacles stand in their way of getting what they want? Does either character get what she wants?

2. The setup here seems simple: two women meet one another in a Starbucks Cafe, they speak, and at the end of the play, one woman leaves the company of the other. What is the story conflict in the play versus the emotional conflict in the play? How does one facilitate the other?

3. What is the moment in the play wherein a red light floods the action about? How does this relate to what Michael Bigelow Dixon describes as "the kick"?

4. How well do you know Sherri and Pauline as characters? Are you sympathetic to their internal conflicts? Why? How does the playwright involve you in their emotional lives?

OFF HAND
by Michel Wallerstein

Characters:

WOMAN (*early 60s*): *Tall, with a commanding presence. Her comments about art are quick and matter of fact. Still attractive. Dressed simply, yet elegant. Wears just the right amount of expensive looking jewelry. There's a nervous energy about her.*

MAN (*late 20s*): *Medium build. Good looking. Charming. Passionate when he talks. Gets easily carried away. He appears to be self-confident but is vulnerable. Dressed in jeans, sweatshirt, and sneakers.*

Setting:
An art gallery in New York City

Lights up on WOMAN looking disapprovingly at a painting stage right (the paintings of the gallery are the audience). She is carrying a catalogue, opens it and stares back straight at the painting.

MAN sits on gallery bench and observes WOMAN. She doesn't see him. She is still looking at the painting in front of her. She frowns.

WOMAN (*Disapprovingly*): Please.

She shrugs and moves on. She now stops (center stage) admiringly in front of the next painting. She clearly likes that one.

WOMAN: Aah! Yes.

She steps back for a better view. MAN approaches WOMAN slowly.

MAN: So you like that one?
WOMAN (*Annoyed, barely looking at him*): Yes.
MAN: It's beautiful.
WOMAN (*Still not quite facing him*): Yes.
MAN: And you like it better than this one?
WOMAN: Without question.
MAN (*Studying the one she likes*): Hmm. What do you like so much about it?
WOMAN: I don't know. I guess how the artist brings her soul to . . .
MAN: . . . her?
WOMAN: (*Matter of fact*): Yes. The artist is a woman.
MAN: Really? How do you know that? (*Reads the signature on the painting*) R. Bastian. R could be for Robert or Ronald or a ton of other names.

WOMAN: I recognize a woman's depth and sensitivity. (*Pointing to the previous painting*) This one, on the other hand, was definitely painted by a man. A man with a dark and twisted vision of our world.

MAN (*Looking closely at the painting; defensive*): At least he signed his full name. Andrew Barton. No ambiguity there.

WOMAN (*Looking at the painting with him*): No soul either. No surprise. Nothing. (*Looking back at the painting she likes*) Whereas this one is filled with substance and meaning . . . It's far too spiritual and inspired to be the work of a man.

MAN: Oh, so Michelangelo or . . . Caravaggio or El Greco—they weren't insightful or spiritual because they were men?

WOMAN: Those great artists lived in different times. A man could not paint like that today. Not in a society only interested in the Dow Jones, MTV, and dot coms . . . Now, if you'll excuse me.

WOMAN *moves to the next painting.* MAN *follows her.*

MAN (*Gentler*): I get carried away sometimes. I didn't mean to come on so strong.

WOMAN (*Kinder*): We're all entitled to our opinions.

MAN: That's right . . . So . . . I'm just curious, how do you know R. Bastian is a woman? There are no pictures in the bio. And no pronouns are ever used to describe her.

WOMAN *now notices* MAN *is attractive.*

WOMAN (*Girlish*): Well, I don't like to brag . . . (*In a loud whisper*) . . . but I know her personally.

MAN: Nothing wrong with a little bragging . . . So what does the R stand for?

WOMAN (*With perfect French pronunciation*): Renée. Renée Bastian.

MAN (*Trying to sound French*): Renée Bastian . . . Hmm? So what do you think Renée's trying to tell us with her painting?

WOMAN *walks back to the previous painting.*

WOMAN: Well I . . . I'm not sure she's trying to tell us anything. The image is . . . magical, almost surreal, like in the early works of Dali. The liberating hand . . .

MAN (*Looking at the painting*): That hand, yes. It's . . . nice.

WOMAN: Nice? It's phenomenal. That hand is power. It's about to liberate the body from its imprisonment, to let it breathe finally, by throwing open the window. The window to freedom, to a new life!

MAN (*Takes a closer look at the painting*): Hmm? Looks to me as if the hand is closing the window, not opening it.

WOMAN: Oh, rubbish! Look at that light. The sun is shining outside that window. There's a gentle, westerly breeze. See how those branches swing gently to the left. And on the oak tree there, a little bluebird is sticking out like in a Rousseau painting.

MAN (*Trying to see*): Oh, yeah. I see it.

WOMAN: . . . And it's chirping.

MAN: You can't really tell it's chirping. It's too small.

WOMAN (*Definite*): It's chirping, alright? I know it is. And it's perfectly clear: the woman in the painting is opening the window. To get air. To begin again. There may be a slight hesitation in the movement, I'll grant you that, but the decision to open that window has been made years ago and now finally, she knows that nothing can stop her anymore. Not even her own fear.

MAN: Oh. So, this is a woman's hand?

WOMAN: Of course it is.

MAN (*Biting*): Don't you think it's kind of square and . . . rugged? And those veins.

WOMAN: Veins?

MAN: You don't see veins like that on a woman's hand.

WOMAN: There are no veins on this hand.

MAN (*Looking closer*): And look, you can even see a few hairs.

WOMAN: Hair! Where?

MAN (*Pointing*): There.

WOMAN: That's no hair. That's just . . . a careless brush stroke.

MAN: More like six or seven . . . No. I'm sorry. That is a man's hand!

WOMAN: This is my hand, okay? I posed for it. She painted *my* hand. (*Places her hand close to the painting*) And there is no hair on *my* hand!

MAN: Lady, this couldn't possibly be your hand.

WOMAN: And why the hell not?

MAN (*Angry*): Look at it. Yours is much prettier than that. So fragile and elegant. This is a hard working, tough hand. But if it's yours, the artist should be shot.

Angry, WOMAN *turns her back to him*.

MAN (*Cont.*): I'm sorry. I got carried away again. A bad habit of mine . . . Let me make it up to you . . . smooth things over with a coffee across the street.

WOMAN: Thank you. I don't think so. I'd just like to enjoy this exhibition. Alone. If you don't mind.

MAN: Of course. I understand. I'm sorry.

WOMAN *walks to the next painting*. MAN *stares at her. She senses it*.

WOMAN (*Faces him*): You're staring.

MAN: Sorry.

WOMAN: It's rude.

MAN: I just find you . . . interesting.

WOMAN: Young man, are you flirting with me?

MAN: Well, you're a very attractive woman.

WOMAN: And . . . almost twice your age. (*Looks at one of the rings on her finger*) If you think I'm one of those rich ladies who spend their time having lunch and attending every gallery opening in town, you're quite mistaken. I'm not rich. These rings are fake. All of them. Not worth a dime.

MAN: Jesus Christ! So now I'm after you for your money?

WOMAN: I'm sorry. I . . . It's just that men your age should be interested in much younger women.

MAN (*Ironic*): Sure. The young should stick together.

WOMAN *shyly walks away. He stares at her again.*

WOMAN: You're staring again. Why?

MAN (*As if caught in a lie*): Habit. I spend a lot of time in places like these and study whoever walks in. I make up stories about them. About their lives. About what brought them in here today.

WOMAN: So, what do you think brought me here today?

MAN: Well, in your case I already know, you came to see your hand.

WOMAN (*Humbled*): Perhaps it isn't my hand.

MAN: So, you didn't pose for it?

WOMAN: I did. Sort of. A friend of mine took pictures of my hand one day. (*Holding her hand out*) He shot two entire rolls. Just of my hand. Imagine that . . . He said that a painter he knew was looking for the hand of perfect elegance and refinement. I was flattered. At my age, I couldn't believe that anything about my appearance could be "perfect." I was thrilled that my friend thought of me, of my hand . . . (*Looks at the painting*) Apparently Renée Bastian didn't agree with him. (*Faces MAN*) But I needed to believe that it was me up there or at least part of me. I've had a hard week. Month. Hell, I've had a hard year and I wanted to feel special today.

MAN: And I blew all that for you, didn't I? Like the asshole, sorry, like the . . . jerk that I am.

WOMAN (*Resigned*): Don't worry about it.

MAN: There's nothing worse than to rob someone of their dream. I know.

WOMAN (*Walking away more decidedly*): It was a small dream. A stupid one.

MAN (*Wanting her attention*): I lied to you.

WOMAN: My dear young man, you haven't known me long enough to lie to me.

MAN: I wasn't really trying to figure you out. When I saw you looking at that painting, with your heart and not your mind, I knew I wanted your response.

WOMAN: Response?

MAN: I'm Andrew Barton. The one with the "dark and twisted vision of the world"?

WOMAN: Oh, dear God!

MAN: I painted the "other" painting. The one you hate.

WOMAN: I . . . I don't really "hate" it, just . . .

MAN: . . . Yes, you do. Everyone does. This is my first exhibition. And I've been watching people ignore my work all week and go straight to R. Bastian's stupid hand—sorry—and since the exhibit ends tonight, I just wanted to know what the hell was wrong with my work? How come no one ever stops in front of *my* painting and goes: "Aah. Yes!"

WOMAN: So I robbed you of *your* dream.

MAN: Yeah, but I'm used to it.

WOMAN: No one ever gets used to that.

MAN: My art teachers told me I was wasting my time, that I should quit art school and get a job.

WOMAN: I'm sure someone must like your work or they wouldn't show it here. Someone obviously believes in you.

MAN: The owner of the gallery is my aunt.

WOMAN *laughs*.

MAN (*Cont.*, *laughing along*): My parents cut me off once they found out I was studying more art than law. So she felt sorry for me. I sold my car, my stereo, my TV, and everything I own just to be able to paint and have this exhibition. Not a good move, I'd say, wouldn't you?

WOMAN: I don't know what to say.

MAN: My mother didn't even show up.

WOMAN (*Gentle*): I'm sure she's sorry.

MAN: You would have shown up, if . . .

He stops, feeling he's gone too far. They look at each other for a short, awkward moment.

WOMAN: You're a nice young man. And I do see some talent in this painting . . .

MAN: . . . despite my dark and twisted vision of the world, huh?

WOMAN (*Looks at his painting*): A great big foot crushing planet Earth? Yes. I'd say it's dark.

MAN: It was meant to be ironic.

WOMAN: You don't say?

There is an awkward silence.

MAN: Sorry you've had such a bad year.

WOMAN (*Hesitant at first*): Well, it's over now. My husband. He was very sick . . . I nursed him day in, day out. I wanted to, of course, but it was very . . . He . . . he finally died last month. Everyone says it's much better this way—no more pain. Maybe for them. My whole world's collapsed . . . as if that foot of yours smashed it to pieces.

Her voice trails off.

MAN: I'm sorry.

WOMAN (*Studies his painting again to avoid eye contact*): Is there . . . Yes! Is there a hand holding that foot?

MAN (*Excited*): I knew it! I knew you'd finally see it. The hand is superimposed on top of the foot, lifting it away and liberating the planet.

WOMAN: And . . . and isn't there someone . . . trying to escape from that crushing foot?

MAN (*Proud*): Yes! That's right.

WOMAN: I think it's a woman . . .

MAN (*Interjects—grinning*): . . . or a man . . .

WOMAN: . . . pulling itself out between the fourth and fifth toe . . .

Of course I wouldn't see the liberating hand if I weren't looking from exactly this angle.

MAN: Exactly!

WOMAN: Very Magritte.

WOMAN *looks at the painting more intensely, then looks away. She seems troubled. She finally faces* MAN *again.*

WOMAN (*Cont., softly*): So the woman is struggling for nothing?

MAN: Or the man. Could be. It could be all in his or her mind. But the liberating hand is definitely a woman's hand. (*Taking her hand gently*) Not unlike yours. As a matter of fact, it's just like yours. (*Looking at her hand closely, then at the painting*) Oh, my God! Of course it's yours.

WOMAN (*Wanting to believe*): Do you think?

MAN: In order to participate in the exhibition, we all had to look at a bunch of pictures that my aunt showed us. I must have seen that photograph your friend took of your hand. And it stood out in my mind and inspired me. (*Pointing triumphantly to his painting*) This is your hand.

WOMAN: Extraordinary. Yes . . . Yes. I . . . I think I do see it. I do . . .

WOMAN *and* MAN *stand closer and look at the painting together.*

Lights Fade.

END OF PLAY

MICHEL WALLERSTEIN ON OFF HAND

In my mind, there are two easy traps to fall into when writing the ten-minute play. The first one is to be too ambitious and try to say too much in too little time. I once saw a ten-minute play that tried to address incest, racism, death of a parent, and an estranged mother and son coming to terms with their pain—all in ten minutes. It's way too much stuff. What resulted was a preachy piece and characters with no humanity whose only purpose was to express the writer's thoughts on these delicate subjects. The second trap is the opposite of the first, where basically the idea is too thin. So . . .

. . . Body parts?! I thought, okay, relax and play along. I chose the hand because it is the most obvious active part of the body (at least on stage). A hand can touch or strike or caress or grab. And you can see it no matter where you sit in the audience. Also, whenever I meet someone, after I've looked in their eyes, I look at their hands. You can tell a lot by someone's hands, but that's another story. My second choice would have been a foot. Ironically, I managed to put it in the play as well . . . Feet can be very erotic, although I'm no fetishist! But I didn't use it in that capacity in the play . . . It's more about the liberating hand versus the crushing foot.

All I knew at first was that my play would be an encounter. I figured, for a ten-minute play, what else could it be but an encounter of some sort? Somehow the idea (which I resisted at first) of a body part made me think of a painting or sculpture. So I decided that the encounter would take place in an art gallery. Then I started thinking about who the people were. The woman came to me faster (female characters always do with me). Once I knew who she was, the reason that she came to the gallery became easier. I then started to write the play, still uncertain of who the other character was going to be, but I knew it would be a man. Things progressed from there.

. . . I like to write about people who meet by chance. People who, if they met in different circumstances, would probably not even notice each other. *Off Hand* is about two such people; they're worlds apart and yet, in ten minutes, they are able to reach out to each other and even help each other nurse their wounds, if only for a moment. Their meeting is the kind of magic you can experience when living in a city like New York.

READER QUESTIONS

1. We've talked about creating interesting behavior for the characters that we write as a means of expressing their emotional lives. What behavior defines these characters? And how does their behavior propel the story forward?

2. One of the structural suggestions I made for writing your ten-minute play is to begin in the middle of the story—forgetting about what we'd all think is a "beginning" and jumping instead right into the

action. How does the playwright do this in *Off Hand*? What's the beginning beat or scene that's missing? How and where do we hear of it later in the play?

3. As people, our choice of words and language often reflects back on our character, histories, education, religion, cultural influences, and age. What do we know, or what can we assume about Man and Woman based solely on their use of language?

4. The hand in the painting is a plot point in the story but also a metaphor for what's not discussed overtly in the play. What does the hand represent between these two people and how is the idea of that woven throughout the story?

PERFECT HAIR
by David Crespy

Characters:

HARRY DENASI, 71, is built like a bull—barrel-chested, massive shoulders and arms, and an impressive gut. He's over seventy, with gorgeous, dark, wavy hair speckled with gray. He sports a white tank top T-shirt, dark pants, no belt. His face is tough, like an old gangster. He's been a jack of all trades, makes dresses, fixes vacuums, and works part-time for the Arsenal. Loves to sing tenor and thinks he's the Messiah.

JASON DENASI, 32, Harry's nephew. A New York magazine editor. Jason's neurotic, insecure, and going through a divorce with small children. He has a wild, thick head of hair.

SAMMY DENASI, 27, Jason's younger brother. Dresses loud, is outrageous, always in debt, and very affectionate. He makes photocopies for a living, and collects bowling shirts. Bald, overweight, glasses, and could give a good goddamn.

Setting:

The bathroom in SAMMY DENASI's one bedroom apartment in Manhattan.

Darkness. A shaft of light falls on HARRY DENASI. *He splashes his hands in a bowl of water, then runs his fingers sensuously through his hair, all the while half-singing a Sinatra number with a velvet tenor.*

HARRY: Fly me to the moon, lah dah, dee dah dee dah dum . . .

As HARRY *lah dee dahs through the song, another shaft of light falls on* JASON DENASI. *He wrestles his own thick shock of hair. It is utterly wild.*

JASON: My Uncle Harry from Brooklyn. He loves his hair. We all do—it's the DeNasi family gift. Thick wavy hair that gets darker and curlier as you get older. It's perfect, almost too perfect, with a life of its own.

SAMMY (O.S., *yelling*): Jason!

HARRY (*Bellows lovingly*): Estelle!

SAMMY (O.S.): Uncle Harry's funeral is like in twenty minutes!

HARRY: Estelle!

SAMMY (O.S.): We need to get on the train! Get out of there!

HARRY: Estelle! Have you been in my bathroom again? Where's my Wildroot? (*Finds it, turns back to his hair*) Never mind! Found it. (*To himself*) She was in here. I can tell. Pretends like she wasn't. (*Grunts, runs his fingers through his hair*) Damn hair.

JASON: Nobody ever went into Uncle Harry's bathroom.

HARRY: Hey, if a man's home is his castle, guess where the throne room is?

JASON: Uncle Harry's secret chamber of hair horrors. As kids, we could hear him cursing from downstairs trying to get it down. And then, somehow, he'd finally do it, slapping at it with Wildroot Hair Tonic. Suddenly he'd be singing, and we're thinking: What the hell is in that stuff?! (*Stands there*) And now at age thirty-two, I finally know why it was so important. But I refuse to use that shit. I've got three degrees. I can get my hair down.

He slaps at his hair. HARRY *smiles, clucks disapprovingly.*

JASON (*Cont.*): I'm going to be late as hell. Concentrate. Get down! Get down! Shit.

HARRY (*To* JASON): Just try it. You don't know until you try it.

JASON *refuses.* HARRY *sighs, splashes the Wildroot in his hand, mixing it with a little water. He dashes it into his hair.*

HARRY (*Cont.*): First you gotta get a feel for the Wildroot in your hands. You mix it with a little water. Not too much—just enough to get the shine. A dab. You touch it to your hair with the tips of your fingers. You see that? Gentle. Mess it up a little. Then you get your brush. Not a comb. You'll lose your hair, you use a comb. And then you do it. You ideally should have two brushes. (*Smacks at his hair with both brushes like a maniac*) See that?!! And you gotta howl at the moon. Like this. (*Howls*) You got that? And then the visions come. I see my mother. Nona. (*Runs his fingers through his loose hair, head back, eyes closed*) And then I like to sing a little Sinatra.

HARRY *gently sings a little Sinatra number, watching* JASON, *then disappears into darkness at the end of Jason's speech.*

JASON: Nona. That's my grandmother. We're Sephardim, from Salonika in Greece. My dad was funny about his hair too. The moment he went in for a meeting, or we went to temple, a wedding, anything, his hand went for . . . a comb. Against Uncle Harry's advice. Dad was a rebel. He was the first to go to college. And worked like a dog! He was sharp and shining and bright. He'd whip out that comb. A few quick swipes. Zip, zip, zip. Like a surgeon. He'd flip it into a pompadour. Perfect. Immaculate. He was a hair genius. But it was weird: his hair stayed so thick and dark and wavy, like Ronald Reagan's, with his face aging underneath it, that it looked kinda freaky. Dad would go into diners, move his hair around for the waitresses, and say, "Hey, doll, is my toupee on right?" Yeah, some- how Dad tamed his hair. But me . . . forget it. (*Struggles with his hair, becoming emotional*) Damn it! Damn!!! Fuck! Get down! Oh, God, look at the time. (*Pause*) Perfect hair is my family's curse.

Lights up on SAMMY's *shining, bald head. He stands behind* JASON.

SAMMY: Well, I personally, could've learned to like it. (*Turns to* JASON) What are you doing?

JASON (*Caught*): Oh, I was just . . .

SAMMY: Talking to the mirror again?

JASON: No, I was . . .

SAMMY: Talking to the mirror again. Psycho.

JASON: Yeah. I guess so. Yes.

SAMMY: It's sad, you know. Pathetic. You live your life like you live in a movie where everything is so wonderful and charming and eccentric.

JASON: Yep. Kinda.

SAMMY: But your life isn't anything like that, Jason. It's pathetic and useless. And I'm only telling you that because I love you and I want you to be a better person.

JASON: What're you? You never even finished college.

SAMMY: I have something you'll never have. Style. And I'm a professional xeroxist. You should see my copies, baby. Clean, hard, crystal clear. (*Pause*) And I cared for my parents before they died. I held them in my arms, you shit. Where the hell were you, Mr. New York Magazine Editor?

JASON: I don't know, Sammy, where was I? Huh? Like maybe struggling with a wife who wanted to dump me. Like watching my life turn to shit.

SAMMY: Look, the services for Uncle Harry start at ten-fifteen and Sandy wants us over there to help with Aunt Estelle. We need to leave NOW.

JASON: I can't take any more funerals, Sammy. I can't take it.

SAMMY: Jason. Don't start. It's not fun for me either, but get used to it because they're all dying. All twelve of them. One big happy Sephardic clan. We laugh together, we drop dead together.

JASON: Alright then, it's Sandy's eulogies. Okay? It's her standing up there, eulogizing.

SAMMY: Leave her alone. She's our older sister and she loves us.

JASON: She's too short to be a Rabbi.

SAMMY: She can't help it if she doesn't look like Madonna.

JASON: She looks like a short man with breasts.

SAMMY: Yeah, well, she's more of a mensch than you'll ever be.

JASON: Oh god, Sammy, I really can't go to Uncle Harry's funeral.

SAMMY (*Rolls his eyes*): What?!

JASON: I can't take any more sadness. (*Pauses*) I miss Mom and Dad. And . . . I'm afraid. I'm afraid . . . (*Combs his hair, but he can't see because of his tears*) This is driving me crazy. Shit.

SAMMY: C'mere, let me do it! Hair is wasted on you. (*As he combs JASON's hair*) God, what I could do with this stuff! I'd be a star. A porn star! (*Vamps to his own bad porn music: "Bomb chick a bomb, bomb chick a bomb." Laughs his head off, then to HARRY*) We didn't all get the fabulous hair, Uncle Harry, now did we?

HARRY reappears with his brushes, smiles at JASON and SAMMY.

JASON: You see him?

SAMMY: Of course. They're all here in my apartment. Old friends.

He waves at HARRY, HARRY waves back.

JASON: Mmm . . . Mom and . . . Dad, too . . . ?

SAMMY: Look, it's rent control, we've all lived here, right?

JASON nods yes weakly, waves to HARRY.

JASON: Well, yes.

SAMMY: Well, duh, it's spook central. And you know what really sucks? They all have that fabulous hair. The wonder hair that thickens with sex and age, and overeating. I had it once, but it was giving me trouble and I told that shit to leave. My theory is: Hair is bad. Remember that. It's nothin' but trouble!

JASON: Sammy, is this supposed to be helping me?

SAMMY: I watched each hair as it left my sweet, little noggin. Each would get this sudden iridescent beauty, all crystalline and nostalgic, and then pop right off to oblivion. Bye, bye, brunette, hello high polish. And it only made me better, more sexy and, alright, a little depressed. But I got over it. I was free. All that hair makes you mean. And sad. Shit, GrandPop had it, and he killed three men with knives.

JASON: But Uncle Harry had that hair. My favorite uncle.

HARRY (*Smiles*): Go on.

JASON: A sweet, gentle guy, who sang tenor, and made nice dresses for ladies.

SAMMY: And eyesights for tanks at the Arsenal, don't forget.

JASON: He killed hundreds of Germans.

SAMMY: With gusto. And he had that little problem.

JASON *and* SAMMY *turn to* HARRY.

HARRY: When you have visions, when you're a messenger of God, the whole world seems like it's unhappy. I see them one day. Two young guys who work with me at the Arsenal, Lou Figurella who works the press, same as his dad, and Vince Harris, a foreman, moping on the train, whining.

SAMMY *and* JASON *become the straphangers,* LOU *and* VINCE. HARRY *reads his paper.*

LOU: They get everything, don't they?

VINCE: The squeaky fuckin' wheel. And for all we do, all we want is a break. No liberation, no human rights. Maybe less taxes. A cute secretary.

LOU: And what do they want? A free ride. Fuckin' nig . . .

HARRY (*Looks up from his paper*): Hey. Hey! You got a job. You shouldn't be saying ugly things about people.

LOU: What? Who are you?

VINCE: What'd he say?

HARRY: Look, I fought the Nazis under Patton. That's what hate gets you.

LOU (*Looks at* JASON *knowingly*): Oh, that must've been very . . .

HARRY: You don't know anything. You're kids. Didn't even go to Vietnam. Right?

VINCE: Look, we're just trying to talk here. So why don' you . . .

HARRY: I'm the messiah.

LOU: What?

HARRY: Nona will tell you. She's in the rosebushes.

VINCE: Rosebushes?

HARRY: I can see everything. Who you are. Who you'll be. Just run your fingers through my hair.

LOU: Like we're going to touch your hair. You've got all that shit in it. No way.

He motions for JASON *to follow him.* JASON *and* SAMMY *exit.*

VINCE: You're fucked up, man. Totally.

HARRY: You don't understand. I know what's going to happen. Please, I know. My mother tells me. I see her in the rosebushes. Please.

SAMMY *appears, walks over to* HARRY, *smiles at him.*

HARRY (*Cont.*): What?

SAMMY (*Sings a la doo-wop*): Bow. Bow. Bow.

HARRY: Oh. Yeah. (*Sings with* SAMMY) Doo wah. Doo wah.

HARRY, SAMMY, *and* JASON *improv a scat doo-wop number of their own choosing—something like "Lovers Never Say Goodbye" by the Flamingos, or "To the Aisle" by The Five Satins—only about hair. After a few bars,* JASON *pulls away.* HARRY *and* SAMMY *continue softly.*

JASON: No one was really sure why Uncle Harry thought he was the messiah.

HARRY: Estelle thought it was because I got a bad case of the runs in Israel . . .

JASON: But it wasn't that.

HARRY: Joel.

JASON: My cousin Joel, Henry's son, died from bone cancer when he was twelve, just before his bar mitzah, with the doctors amputating a different part of him each month, trying to save him. And he was such a sweet kid, I remember. He'd be hopping around on his crutches, trying to play football.

HARRY: Joel.

JASON: They loved him so much. And it was so horrible when Joel died. We all just think it was easier for Uncle Harry to think he was the Messiah than to think God had taken Joel for no reason at all.

SAMMY: Oh, God. Shut up with that shit. He was crazy, that's all!

HARRY: Maybe a little.

JASON *goes back to struggling with his hair.*

JASON: Damn it. It just won't . . .

SAMMY (*While HARRY continues to quietly sing*): Why do you always have to make things more complicated than they really are? Jason, we all cope any way we can. What do you think I did all those years when you and Mom and Dad thought I was a failure? How do you think I felt when I had to drop out of college and you got a Ph.D.? I bought some Hawaiian shirts. Some Italian shoes. A diamond, sapphire pinky ring. Little things.

JASON: Little expensive things.

SAMMY: We all do whatever we have to do to cope. Mostly we hang onto each other and treat each other kindly. Right? We've got to go. It's our responsibility.

JASON: You go without me.

SAMMY: No, we're all going. It's Uncle Harry's funeral for God's sake. It's Uncle Harry.

JASON: Alright! Alright!

With a sudden burst of energy, he rushes to the sink, squirts a tube of something in his hands, dashes it through his hair. He tries to brush it, but something is wrong.

JASON (*Cont.*): Oh, God. What is this? I can't take this!

SAMMY: Don't pull that shit again. What did you do? (*Picks up tube, looks at it*) This is Pepsodent, you nimrod. Hello? Get that out of your hair! What is wrong with you?

JASON: I can't. I can't take anymore. Elizabeth is divorcing me. All this death. And I see my kids an eighth of the time. I can't even fucking brush my hair. (*Struggling*) I don't understand. Why is my wife leaving me? I don't get it.

JASON collapses, brush in hand.

SAMMY (*Holding him up*): Jason. Jason! C'mon. You've got those beautiful boys. Do you know how many people would love to have those kids? Do you know how much I would? Pull yourself together. (*JASON bawls*) Look . . . Oh, shit . . . Don't make me do this. Every fucking time. Alright. Alright. Look . . . I love you, Jason. I really do.

JASON: Yeah?

SAMMY: I do. So does Sandy. And mom and dad loved you too. So did Uncle Harry.

JASON: You think so?

SAMMY: C'mon, brush your hair already.

JASON: It's sticking up everywhere. (*Turns to SAMMY, takes his hand a moment*) Sammy.

HARRY: Here, take this. You know what to do. Two brushes.

HARRY hands JASON a bottle of Wildroot. JASON looks at HARRY, then at SAMMY. Silence.

JASON: Wildroot. Shit. (*Taking it*) What the hell is in this stuff?

SAMMY: We do what we can, Jason. Right?

JASON *tentatively wets his hands, runs it through his hair. Opens the Wildroot, splashes it on his hands, and slap-rubs them together—looking at his hands with a kind of terror. He looks to* HARRY *and* SAMMY *for support. Both* HARRY *and* SAMMY *shrug and smile.* JASON *dashes the Wildroot through his hair, wincing, then giving into the feeling.* JASON *starts to brush his hair, both brushes. The hair responds, and* JASON *becomes more confident.* SAMMY *and* HARRY *suddenly* HOWL! JASON *joins them, howling tentatively then with vigor, brushing faster and with some nerve. He smiles.*

JASON: Holy shit! It works!

SAMMY *and* HARRY *broadly smile, start to sing behind him—an Elvis number. They both pop on a fake Elvis hairpiece. They both brush combs over their heads, singing.* JASON *sings along with them. All three sing and brush (or comb) their hair passionately as the music swells in the background.*

LIGHTS FADE on their smiling faces.

END OF PLAY

DAVID CRESPY ON PERFECT HAIR

Well, the body part thing started to freak me, because I'm very sensitive about my appearance. When I look in the mirror I see Drew Carey looking back at me. I'm built in a kind of pear shape, with a butt that seems to be most of my body! . . . I went to see Suzan-Lori Parks' *Venus* and I thought it was the story of my life—a woman who's a freak because of her butt! So the body thing was definitely a bit nervous-making.

However, I decided to focus on this little tic I have, this reaction to stress and terror, which is my somewhat constant neurotic combing. I've pulled way back since high school, but it's still there when I'm nervous. My Dad did the same thing, and it's because we were blessed with this lump or helmet of hair that seems to have its own life. I'm never able to keep it down, and when I do, it looks so canned . . . So I decided to futz around with my hair and this little problem I've had for years in a play script. All of my uncles solved the problem with hair grease, but being a child of the seventies, I didn't do the hair grease thing. And my younger brother Jonathan, who has very little hair, seems so much more together than I am (and generally makes fun of me). Hence my theory that men with hair are actually at a greater disadvantage—hair is a sign of failure and pain. And that was the seed for my play.

[The play] started with an image of my uncle, this bear of a guy, who always frightened me as a kid, brushing his hair, slapping on the Dixie Pomade. He's really a blend of several uncles, most of whom were Teamsters and had a kind of brute elegance to them. They were all Sephardic Jewish men, who were very demonstrative and loving. All the men in my family kissed each other. It was sometimes a bit horrifying to have my Uncle Dave grab you by the ears and give you a big, wet, nasty, hairy kiss, but it happened at every greeting, and these were men who enjoyed life to the fullest . . . There was such an odd mix to these men, terrible tempers and intense furies, mingled with carefully coifed hair and manicured nails.

. . . So here I was with this character and I needed a situation, which again readily presented itself. I remembered that I had had an emotional collapse at the death of one of my uncles. I was not on speaking terms with my family at the time, and I was having a hard time trying to make sense of the whole mess. I just couldn't get myself dressed for the event, knowing I had to face my family, my life, all the problems in my marriage. It all gelled to this one point in my life when I just couldn't get my hair to sit on my head the right way . . . So these two events collided and became the world of the play.

READER QUESTIONS

1. What elements in *Perfect Hair* are theatrical, and what structural or dramaturgical purpose do they serve? Are the doo-wop songs just doo-wop songs? Or do they in some way intensify what's emotionally at stake for Jason?

2. There are three perspectives on one object, hair, in the development of the play. How do these perspectives push the action forward in the play and bring the conflict to a satisfying resolution?

3. All central characters in our plays take a journey that brings them emotionally from one place to another by the play's end. Where does Jason start emotionally, and where does he end? More importantly, what happens in the middle of the play that makes Jason's journey almost inevitable?

4. The character of Sammy is practically the dramatic antithesis of his brother, Jason. How do their unparallel lives work together to justify the dramatic arc of the play?

E D F C Z P
by Wendy Yondorf

Characters:

DR. GOLDBERG, male, 70s. An ophthalmologist, speaks with a lisp. Loves his profession.

MRS. DAGABI, female, 70s. A widow, retired. Nervous, high strung.

Setting:

A doctor's office. There is a chair at center and a counter DS right. On top of the counter: a water pitcher, paper cups, medicines, drops, patients' charts, a bowl of candy. On a lower shelf are some needles, syringes, and more medicines. A large, old-fashioned eye chart is visible.

Note: Doctor's Goldberg's lisp should be ever-present.

LIGHTS UP. DOCTOR GOLDBERG, *wearing a white lab coat, sits in the patient chair. He reads a medical journal. MRS. DAGABI enters the office, unnoticed by DR. GOLDBERG. She is well-dressed, carries a handbag, and uses a walking cane. MRS. DAGABI peers about the office and addresses the eye chart.*

MRS. DAGABI: The nurse said to enter here?

DR. GOLDBERG *rises quickly from the chair.*

DR. GOLDBERG: Ah! Good afternoon. I'm Doctor Goldberg, and you mutht be . . . (*Checks in a patient chart*) Mrs. Da-Gabby?

MRS. DAGABI (As *if correcting an idiot*): Dagabi! (*Pronounced: dah-gah-BEE*) Could I have a seat, doctor?

DR. GOLDBERG (*Unfailingly polite*): I'm tho sorry—I think it might be easiest if I ethcort you. (*Taking her elbow*) Right thith way . . . good, good—

MRS. DAGABI *draws her elbow away from him and sits.*

MRS. DAGABI (*Plops into chair*): I can see!
DR. GOLDBERG: Probably not ath well as you'd like to. Glaucoma theverely limits the peripheral vision.
MRS. DAGABI: Don't you think I know that?
DR. GOLDBERG: I don't think we've met before . . .
MRS. DAGABI: We have not.
DR. GOLDBERG: Tho! We're going to give you a little laser therapy for your glaucoma?
MRS. DAGABI: Not if you keep chattering.
DR. GOLDBERG: Would you like a bit of water or a peppermint?

Doctor offers her a bowl of mints.

MRS. DAGABI (*Sharp*): I don't care for sweets!
DR. GOLDBERG (*Teasing*): Don't care for, or, watching your figure?
MRS. DAGABI: Who the hell offers candy to patients anymore? . . . You don't seem terribly spry, Doctor, how old are you?
DR. GOLDBERG (*Chuckles*): Well, I've been practicing medicine for a few score yearth. Who would you rather have, a young whipper snapper jutht out of medical school, or a nicely aged practitioner?
MRS. DAGABI: I'd rather have Brad Pitt. But my grandson is visiting me in a week and I'd like to know what the hell he looks like. He's the only relative I have.
DR. GOLDBERG: Well, this is a big occasion! How old is this grandthon—?

She grasps at the doctor's sleeve and pulls him to her.

She trembles with fear.

MRS. DAGABI: I want you to tell me exactly what you're going to do, before you do it. You tell me step by step: you say, I'm going to shine a light on your left eye and *then* you shine it. That's how we're going to proceed, all right?

DR. GOLDBERG: OK.

MRS. DAGABI: And there will be no need for injections, correct?

DR. GOLDBERG: None whatthoever. I perform at leatht thix to eight of these procedures daily. You're in expert handth. But before we turn on the laser, I'd like to examine your eyeth.

MRS. DAGABI (*Shrieks suddenly*): I need a glass of water!

DR. GOLDBERG (*Taken aback, but his voice remains calm*): Certainly.

DR. GOLDBERG *fetches her a cup of water as* MRS. DAGABI *feels for a bottle of pills in her purse. She grabs the cup of water from him and swallows three pills in a gulp.*

DR. GOLDBERG: What are you taking?!

MRS. DAGABI: They're mine! (*Clutching the bottle to her chest*) They're aspirin, for Chrissake! I take them for headaches!

DR. GOLDBERG: All right. Slow down. If you need a thedative, I'd rather give you one and not have to guess what you're taking.

MRS. DAGABI: I don't need anything. (*Hiccups*) . . . Excuse me . . . (*Hiccups again*) Just ignore me, I'm fine.

DR. GOLDBERG (*Kindly*): Take some deep breaths.

He demonstrates, encouraging her—she follows, reluctantly. She begins hiccupping, he suddenly sneezes.

MRS. DAGABI: Gesundheit.

DR. GOLDBERG: Danke schon.

MRS. DAGABI (*Abrupt*): Do you speak German?

DR. GOLDBERG: No. Do you?

MRS. DAGABI: No.

DR. GOLDBERG: You know, thith is an elective procedure, there's no reason to force yourself to do it today, Mrs. Bag-uh-dung—

MRS. DAGABI (*Outraged*): Dah-gah-BEE! It's not Goldberg or Smith, but it's my name. Happens to be African.

DR. GOLDBERG: Mrs. Dagabi, I'm not sure you're in a good place—

MRS. DAGABI: My grandson arrives in four days from Australia. So let's get this thing going.

DR. GOLDBERG: Ath you wish. You're the boss.

MRS. DAGABI: I've had nine appointments for this procedure and walked out nine times. I don't like doctors.

DR. GOLDBERG (*Chummy*): You know what? I'm thcared thtiff of my dentist. I think the man actually enjoys inflicting pain.

MRS. DAGABI (*Proudly*): Oh! I never go to the dentist!

DR. GOLDBERG: It'th a primitive form of medithine. Thith procedure, however, is one of the modern miracleth of science. You will feel nothing! And yet, in the blink of an eye—you'll regain your full scope of vision!

MRS. DAGABI: Sounds too good to be true.

DR. GOLDBERG: I should warn you, it can be very dithorienting. Clarity is a formidable enterprise. You will thee the panorama of trash in the street, the maple leaf's toothy edges, the breadth of the Hudson River, the line of your grandthon's chin—

MRS. DAGABI: Let's not be so grand, doctor, I got two bad eyes and you got a machine to help me out. . . . What's first?

DR. GOLDBERG: A very thimple, old-fashioned eye tetht.

The doctor points to a row of large letters on the eye chart just below the big E.

DR. GOLDBERG (*Cont.*): Pleathe tell me the letterth you see on thith row.

MRS. DAGABI (*Cranes her neck forward, and reads the line perfectly*): E-D-F-Thee-Z—I'm sorry! (*Shakes her head, reddens*) E-D-F-C-Z-P.

DR. GOLDBERG: Exthellent. I want you to look at my face, *directly* at my face and tell me how many fingers I'm holding up on my left and right handth.

The doctor steps just a few feet away from her. He holds his hands wide apart, one showing three fingers the other five.

MRS. DAGABI: Can't see a thing except kind of a big hazy halo around your head.

The doctor jots some notes in her chart. He pulls a penlight from his pocket.

DR. GOLDBERG: I'd like to look at your eyeth a little more closely. May I shine a thmall light in your eye?

She nods, tense. The doctor looks very closely at each of her eyes using his pocket light. He seems fascinated.

DR. GOLDBERG (*Cont.*): Interethting. You have two different colored irises—

MRS. DAGABI *kicks the doctor, hard, in the shin. He howls in pain.*

DR. GOLDBERG (*Cont.*): Ahhhhh! Damn it to hell!
MRS. DAGABI: I'm sorry—! I didn't mean to—it was an automatic reaction!
DR. GOLDBERG (*Rubbing his leg, obviously in real pain*): Wath it?!
MRS. DAGABI: Yes!
DR. GOLDBERG (*Irate*): Well, it still hurth!
MRS. DAGABI: Oh, please, don't be angry with me, Doctor—!
DR. GOLDBERG: I have been a practitioner for over forty yearth; not once have I been struck until today.
MRS. DAGABI: I'm so sorry, doctor! You don't understand. I'm so terribly frightened! The thought of— And yet, I can't abide this fuzzy, damn grey world!
DR. GOLDBERG: I know you're frightened. You took some librium a few minuteth ago. That's a very powerful thedative.

Pause.

MRS. DAGABI: Why didn't you have that lisp corrected? It infantalizes you.

DR. GOLDBERG: Ith that tho? Most of my patients tell me I thound exactly like Brad Pitt.

MRS. DAGABI (*Cracks up, laughing*): Good one! Very good . . . But seriously, Doctor, how did you get such a bad lisp?

DR. GOLDBERG (*Suddenly, angry*): Where did you get your name, Mrs. *Mandela*?

MRS. DAGABI (*Wide-eyed*): I asked you first.

DR. GOLDBERG: I asked you thecond.

MRS. DAGABI: Oh! You're an immature old bugaboo!

DR. GOLDBERG: Yeth, but a charming one. And single, too. (*They laugh*) Here'th my theory. You're on the lam, thee, and Dagabi ith your ingeniouth aliath.

MRS. DAGABI: It isn't an alias, it's a code. Dagabi is the alphabetic equivalent for my identification number: four, one, seven, one, two, nine. D is the fourth letter, A the first, and so on. . . . I had the number removed, but there are things you don't entirely want to forget.

DR. GOLDBERG: My God. You were in the concentration camps? (*Beat*) But you must have been a child!

MRS. DAGABI: I was. You weren't in the war, were you, Doctor?

DR. GOLDBERG (*Frowning*): Flat feet and tunnel vision kept me right here . . . Not exactly a shining moment in my perthonal history. . . . Pleathe, tell me your thtory, Mrs. Dagabi.

MRS. DAGABI: I had four eye operations—without any anesthesia.

DR. GOLDBERG: Eye operationth—? Whatever for?

MRS. DAGABI: They were "experimenting" with eye color.

DR. GOLDBERG: Oh, my poor dear—!

MRS. DAGABI: I had it easy compared to my sister.

DR. GOLDBERG: Excuse me, I thought . . . You thaid your grandthon was your only relative?

MRS. DAGABI: I *had* a twin sister, Leah. They took a particular interest in her. She always got more sweets than me—I think because she was the prettier one. They left her eyes alone, but, two of the surgeries in her spinal cord left her paralyzed. She couldn't walk or talk after those procedures. On her fifth surgery they took out her sex organs. She didn't survive that one. We were twins. We were twelve.

DR. GOLDBERG (*Shaking his head*) God in heaven. . . . You mutht be one of the latht of the Mengele twinth.

MRS. DAGABI: I am the last. (*Beat*) You see, I'm not a crackpot, Doctor. I'm just a frightened old woman.

DR. GOLDBERG: On the contrary, it was very brave of you to come here, Mrs. Daga—

MRS. DAGABI (*Shy*): It's Schnee. Alma Schnee.

DR. GOLDBERG (*Taking her hand in his*): The nightmare is behind you. Dr. Mengele ith long dead.

MRS. DAGABI: He died, well into his eighties, peacefully by the seashore.

DR. GOLDBERG: Tho much evil in one man . . . Of courthe, he must have had assithtanths, too.

MRS. DAGABI: Yes. A few assistants. Boys, really, not much older than Leah and me. One of the boys did the injections and drew blood, daily. From the neck. And, of course the fool wasn't very skilled.

DR. GOLDBERG (*Ironic*): Jutht another Nazi, following orderth, eh?

MRS. DAGABI: Yes, a favorite SS line of defense.

DR. GOLDBERG: You are an extraordinary person. I feel honored to have met you, Alma Thnow.

MRS. DAGABI: *Schnee*, not Snow.

DR. GOLDBERG: Oh! Padon me—

MRS. DAGABI: Schnee is the German word for Snow. You told me that you don't speak German.

DR. GOLDBERG (*Coyly bragging*): I'm a highly educated man, Mrs.—

MRS. DAGABI (*Growing paranoid*): Do you know the Japanese word for snow? (*Pause*) Why don't you answer me?

DR. GOLDBERG: I do have other appointmeths today, Mrs.—

MRS. DAGABI: Where were you born, Dr. Goldberg?

DR. GOLDBERG: Thaint Paul, Minnethota, and believe me, I grew up knee deep in Schnee. (*Beat*) Now, Alma, shall we protheed?

MRS. DAGABI (*Frantic*): No! I don't want to. (*Accusing*) You're not from Minnesota.

DR. GOLDBERG *turns away from her and moves to the counter, DS. He prepares a syringe.*

DR. GOLDBERG: My dearetht Alma, you're overwrought—

MRS. DAGABI: GET THE NURSE!

He approaches her with the syringe, held low.

DR. GOLDBERG: Now, now. Thith ith justh a mild thedative—

He swabs her arm with a cotton ball. She struggles to pull away.

MRS. DAGABI: I don't need one!

Deftly, he administers the injection.

DR. GOLDBERG: There, there. Breathe normally. (*He demonstrates*) That'th right. I'm right here.

MRS. DAGABI's *breathing slows. She relaxes.*

DR. GOLDBERG (*Cont.*): That'th better. And when you thay tho, I'll have the nurthe ethcort you to the lather room.

DR. GOLDBERG *disposes the syringe.*

MRS. DAGABI: Yes! Robert must see his Alma, strong and clear . . . You won't tell him about my—my little fright attack, will you, Doctor?

DR. GOLDBERG (*Kindly*): No, my dear, of courth, not.

MRS. DAGABI's *head slumps to the side, her eyes wide open.* DR. GOLD-BERG *checks her pulse. He speaks without his lisp.*

DR. GOLDBERG: Your secret is safe with me.

Lights fade.

END OF PLAY

WENDY YONDORF ON E D F C Z P

Two weeks before the deadline, I took out a pad and stared at it. I fantasized about this being the ten-minute play that would—what?—be the first ten-minute play to be produced on Broadway to be followed by a full-length, ten-minute feature film production. I thought, Yondorf, you're a twit if you don't write the best damn ten minutes you can. But first . . . a body part . . .

A week before the deadline I was riding the M66 cross town bus and for no particular reason, the gas-permeable contact lens in my right eye slid up and back under my upper eyelid. I knew I shouldn't try to retrieve the thing because: (1) I'd probably drop it, and (2) I'd gross out the gross teenager sitting next to me who was pulling on his nose ring. So, I tried not to think about the incredibly uncomfortable feeling of the lens scraping on my eyeball surface. I flashed on being eight years old and watching my older sister being fitted for contact lenses. The doctor insisted there was no discomfort and she should stop grabbing at her lid and crying so much. And then the story of an eye doctor who loves his work but who has a sadistic streak unfolded in my mind.

The evening of my crosstown bus ride, I took out a pencil and recycled paper and made a pact to write down the whole idea and finish a draft, however rough. I wrote the setting—an ophthalmologist's office—and then got stuck on the names of the characters. Forty-eight hours later I sent a draft to two friends and they made it clear that the whole thing was vague, absurd, and the ending was not an ending. I tried to like the idea of vague and absurd. I rewrote the thing another eight times . . .

. . . I wanted to explore evil in a banal setting. I wanted to take our assumptions about a routine, fairly normal event in life and turn it on its head. I was daunted and excited by the task of beginning with this innocent event (an eye procedure) and arriving at the end in a place of horror. I didn't set out to write a horror story but that evolved when I began to think about why this glaucoma visit for the woman character was so charged. I also was interested in the doctor's perfect disguise. (I have to give credit to Hannah Arendt's book *Eichmann in Jerusalem*, in which she exposes the theme "the banality of evil.") Having said all this, my overriding goal was to push the comic limits of the event and have the horror of the ending delayed to the last possible second.

READER QUESTIONS

1. When talking about the ten-minute play, Judith Royer (p. 57) said that it seemed to be most effective when the characters in the play were subtle and complex. How does the playwright achieve this in E D F C Z P?

2. You might say the simple story line of the play is whether Dr. Goldberg will win the confidence of Mrs. Dagabi in order to have a successful eye procedure. We know better than that. So what details in the story begin nagging you that there is actually something much larger at stake?

3. What do you find comic in the play? How does it work in balance to the drama? And what does it do to the overall momentum and arc of the play?

4. This is a traditional three-part structured play with exposition, rising action layered with complications, crisis, and climax. Can you identify those parts of the play? How does one lead to the other?

HAIRSTORY
by Tish Benson

Characters:

(Child) BERTA: 9 *years old and* (Adult) BERTA: 21 *years old, played by the same actress.*

MOMMA: *Late 30s.*

THE EXTRAS: *Three or four chorus girls with Pointer Sisters' style, wearing colorful outfits and outrageous hairdos. (The EXTRAS can be used throughout the story as long as they don't disturb the story, but add to it.)*

Setting:

The kitchen. A large sink. Nearby is a chair with telephone books in it. A table next to it with ten different shampoos. Center stage is another table with home-made hair products and an electrical burner with two hot combs on top. A small TV and radio nearby.

The Play:

This is a memory play. Visually and with sound effects, it should be interpreted as if by a nine-year-old child with an overactive imagination. Oversized animated cutouts of combs, boxes of hair oil, shampoos, and any other colorful exaggerated props will suit this play. The characters are Southern, yes, but campy/coonish, no. Please allow the characters to be realized as humans and not as caricatures or stereotypes.

Lights put ADULT BERTA in a circle.

(Adult) BERTA: At age five with folks all the time starin down at me askin momma was that my real hair . . . was all that hair on my head mine . . .

THE EXTRAS (*Bop around, singing like a 60s girls group*): Is all that hair on her head hers?
Is all that hair on her head hers?
Is all that hair on her head hers!

BERTA: I was more of a display than a me. Momma would stand on her pedestal . . .

Lights on MOMMA. She is atop a huge bolder, holding the biggest blackest comb known to woman in one hand and a gallon jug labeled, "Mommas Secret Hair Growing Grease" in the other.

BERTA: . . . lift her torch affirming the pride that most mothers felt when people gloated over their child. An inner thing that cause of our connection—umbilical cords are never really broken—I saw clear.

THE EXTRAS (*Encircling* MOMMA): Is all that hair on her head hers? Is all that hair on her head hers?
Is all that hair on her head hers!

MOMMA: Yeah, it's hers and I got all the broken nails to prove it. It's like wire . . . her hair can cut ya and it takes forever to wash. I wouldn't wish hair like hers on my worst enemy . . . problems, forever problems.

THE EXTRAS: Oh but it's so pretty—
It's so thick.
It's so pretty.
It's so thick
pretty! thick! pretty! thick! pretty! thick! pretty! thick! (*Beat*) What do u use on it?

MOMMA: A strong black comb . . . I said a Strong Black Comb. Can't get one of them little pink combs with the teeth close together . . . naw that ain't gone do it . . . and the Strong Black Comb gotta have wide teeth. So it's gotta be wide and it's gotta be strong . . .

THE EXTRAS (*Chanting*): It's gotta be wide and it's gotta be strong it's gotta be wide and it's gotta be strong wide-n-strong-wide-n-strong . . .

MOMMA: And I keep it oiled real good with my secret hair grease.

THE EXTRAS (*One yells, the others whisper*): Secret Hair Grease! . . . it's a secret . . . Secret Hair Grease! . . . it's a secret . . . Secret Hair Grease! . . . shhhhhh . . . it's a secret . . .

(Adult) BERTA: Momma's secret hair grease . . . it musta worked. Or maybe it was the massages and the chants . . .

THE EXTRAS and MOMMA (*Chanting*): Grow grow grow grow grow grow grow . . .

EXTRA 1 *mimes massaging* EXTRA 2's *head while* EXTRA 3 *parades around the stage displaying kidlike drawings of long hair ads.* MOMMA *continues chanting.*

(Adult) BERTA: . . . cutouts . . . pages and pages of long hair ads from Ebony, Jet, and Essence magazines . . . maybe it was all of that . . . maybe it was just the belief that it would work.

MOMMA: Pretty hair pretty hair grow grow grow . . .

MOMMA *continues her chant until* BERTA *is nine years old.*

(Adult) BERTA: At age five, folks staring down at me . . .
EXTRA 1: At age six staring down . . .
EXTRA 2: Age seven . . .
EXTRA 3: Eight, starin' down . . .
THE EXTRAS: Age nine—
MOMMA (*Sweet singsongy voice*): BERTA!

Thunder sound. Lights flash.

Lights up. BERTA *at nine years old sits. She is forever getting her hair done by* MOMMA.

BERTA: Momma why u gotta put this stinky stuff on my hair?
MOMMA: Momma know it don't smell good, but it works . . . baby, look how long and thick yo hair is.
BERTA: What's in it that makes it smell like that?
MOMMA: I put special ingredients. Don't worry about what they are. I'm ya momma. I ain't tryin to kill ya, so be still. (*Beat*) Girl! Yo hair just soak up oil . . . now I just greased this side of yo scalp and just look at it! Already dry.
BERTA: Don't put no mo' on my hair momma . . . everybody be laughin' at me callin' me stank head.
MOMMA: Callin' you what!? Who? Tell me . . .
BERTA: Forget it, momma.
MOMMA: Baby, how you gone care what some little chicken-headed jealous gals gone say . . . ain't got no mo' hair than a pop . . . got tha' nerve to talk about my baby. Well I'm goin' up there to that damn school tomorrow . . . seem like them little witches got too much time on they hands if they all up in yo head . . .

BERTA: Just forget it momma . . . it ain't all them anyway . . . I know . . .

MOMMA: Berta, everywhere we go somebody sayin' somethin' about how nice yo hair is and you ain't grateful. All this work I do to keep yo hair up—

BERTA: Forget it, momma . . .

MOMMA: When I was growin' up I had to do my own hair and ya Aunt Vee-Vee's hair. My momma didn't have time and I ain't got time neither but I make time and here you are showing me how ungrateful yo ass is.

BERTA: Can I turn on the TV?

MOMMA: You can't hardly hold a good head now . . . you tryin to look at TV . . . it just ain't gone work.

BERTA: Well can we have the radio on?

MOMMA: Okay . . .

BERTA *snaps. The radio turns on.*

MOMMA: But don't change the channel.

Aretha Franklin sings. MOMMA *starts singing louder than the radio.* BERTA *is bored.*

BERTA: Momma, u almost through?

MOMMA (*Singing loud*): "Now I don't mind company . . . cause company is alright every once in a while . . . I sayed I don't mind company cause company is alright every once in a while."

She finishes the entire song, dancing around the kitchen singing in BERTA's *face until* BERTA *finally loosens up and joins her mother. Duet style. Yes, they carry on. Song ends. This Hallmark moment ends.*

EXTRA 3 (as RADIO ANNOUNCER): That was the forever queen of soul.

BERTA *and* MOMMA *resume the "doing hair" positions.*

BERTA: Momma, why didn't you ever try to be a real singer?

MOMMA: Oh? So you don't call that real singing?

BERTA: You know what I mean, momma . . . see you coulda been on TV . . . we coulda been rich!

MOMMA: I'm as rich as I need to be.

She tests the hot comb. It's hot. She hot combs BERTA's *hair.*

BERTA: But we coulda had money, momma . . . or maybe you shoulda been a hairdresser . . . cause you like doin hair . . .

MOMMA: No, I don't either!

Upset, she stops doing BERTA's *hair.*

MOMMA: You think I like doing yo hair? Well I don't!

MOMMA *becomes dreamy.* THE EXTRAS *sing a soft hula.*

MOMMA: I'd love to just be "chillin" . . . out on a tropical island with some cocktail and coconut juice in it . . . that's what I'd like to be doin . . .

BERTA: All I was trying to say is you do hair good, momma, and that's another way we could be rich . . .

MOMMA: That'll be yo job . . . (*Resumes hot combing her hair*) if that's what you want Berta you can have that . . . you can have it . . . (*Beat*) Damn Girl! You hold a bad head! Look down! That means ya eyes are supposed to look down . . . every time you raise ya eyes ya raise ya head. That's how you gone get burned one of these days. These combs are hot girl and the way you jerking and moving . . . looking up when you supposed to be lookin down . . . that's how come nobody else like to do yo hair . . . I end up having to tip 'um real big cause you hold such a bad head . . .

BERTA (*Interrupts*): Alright! Momma . . . look I'm holdin my head down . . . see! See! It's down, ok?

Lights fade. Lights up MOMMA *on the telephone in the kitchen.* BERTA *getting her hair done.*

MOMMA: Yeah, girl, I got time. I'm just fixin Berta's hair and bout to make some short bread . . . yeah . . . be ready in no time . . . I'll get this gal of mine to brang yall over some just as soon as they done . . . chile, she's smellin herself real strong these days . . . forever talkin back. I don't know . . . I'm hopein this a phase cause I don't know if I can take too much of this back talk of hers. Girl, could you imagine us questionin' anything momma sayed or did! Can you imagine! This girl got lip for everything.

EXTRA 3 (*Gossiping to* EXTRA 2): She ain't got no reason to complain . . .

MOMMA: Now she ain't but nine and here she is always—

EXTRA 2: Mmmmhuh, all her life she wanted a little girl . . .

EXTRA 1: To fix her hair, buy her cute dresses . . .

EXTRA 3: AND, fix her hair . . .

MOMMA: On and on, from one thing to the next with this one here . . . what a difference a year makes . . . last time this year, Berta ain't question nothin' I said or did . . . now, it's from one sassy thing to the next . . .

THE EXTRAS (*Break out in girlie chant*): She wanted a lil' girl to fix her hair, fix her hair, fix her hair, she wanted a lil' girl to fix . . .

BERTA: Momma!

MOMMA: Berta, can't you see . . . I'm talkin to ya auntie.

BERTA: Can't you get off for me . . . yo only daughter in the whole wide world?

MOMMA: See, girl, I told ya tha world revolves around this one here. Everbody is supposed to stop whatever they doing and see about her . . . ain't that some shit!

Lights down. Lights up on THE EXTRAS. *They are nine years old.*

EXTRA 1: Let's play teams now.

EXTRA 2: We can't. We need somebody else.

EXTRA 3: There's Berta. Let's go ask her.

EXTRA 1: Forget her. Her momma thanks she's better than anybody. They both make me sick.

EXTRA 2: I feel like throwin up on both of um.

THE EXTRAS *make gagging noises.*

BERTA: Momma!

MOMMA: I'm tellin ya, girl, you definetly made the right choice . . . not get ya self tied down to ungratefullness . . . I've made up my mind right after this hair show, I'mma turn her hair over to her . . . I'm too old to be dealin with that bad head child . . . the only reason I'm gettin her ready is cause her daddy already paid the entry fee and bought her this pretty out-fit . . . yeah, girl, after this show I'm tellin u tha truth, I'm wipin my hands of this fixin her hair . . .

BERTA: Momma, I don't wanna get my hair done, it hurts.

MOMMA: Hair don't hurt girl (*Beat*) A good washin' will do you good.

BERTA: But didn't u say my hair grow in dirt like wild flowers.

MOMMA: Yeah but everythang need some washin, baby.

MOMMA *washes* BERTA's *hair, scrubbing and pulling, wearing poor* BERTA *out.*

MOMMA (*Beat*): Damn that's my fourth nail . . . yo hair cut like wire girl.

BERTA: I'm tired my neck hurt . . . when you gone be through?

MOMMA: Girl, I got this whole other side of yo head to do. We ain't half finished.

BERTA: Let's stop and do it tomorrow.

MOMMA: Tomorrow? Tomorrow is the big hair show . . . If we win this year we go into The Hair Hall of Fame.

THE EXTRAS: Ooooooohhhhh.

MOMMA: Nobody around in this area won three times straight and

I've seen these little incha hair gals that's tryin to win . . . they mommas thank that all them bows gone count for the real thang . . . and them weave headed children . . . ump-ump-ump . . . (*Beat*) This yo glory, girl. Don't forget that a woman's hair is her glory.

MOMMA *atop her big boulder.* THE EXTRAS *parade around holding up outrageous cutouts.*

MOMMA: This was the first time we won the hair show. I fixed Berta's hair up like the leanin Tower of Pisa . . . took about 4 hours . . . and this one I called Sassy Betty Boop cause I had it slick to her head and the tendrils comin down in the front but the back had these oodles of curls . . . so it was sassy and this one I called Farrah circa 1970s . . . This year I'mma do something real special (*Whispers*) . . . Berta's hair gone be like a fisherman's net. I'mma crochet it with shells and beads . . . ahh, it's gone be so pretty. I dreamt it up . . . I'm gone call it—The Littlest Mermaid.

Lights flash. BERTA *sits on the chair. She is leaned all the way back at the kitchen sink.* MOMMA *washes her hair.* EXTRA 1 *calls out the stuff on the table like they are inspector #12.*

EXTRA 1: . . . two . . . huge pickle barrels filled with warm water . . .
EXTRA 2: . . . industrial size containers of shampoo and conditioner, three eggs, a cup of hot oil . . .
EXTRA 1: . . . a small bowl to scoop the water; Saran Wrap for the heat pack . . .
EXTRA 3: Momma is on her third full wash sweatin and gruttin like she just picked a full bale of cotton and baked five pies for Miss Suzy's Women's Suffrage Church Social Tea and Bake Sale.
BERTA: You ain't thru yet? Momma my back hurt . . . can I raise up?
MOMMA: This the last one. Yo hair was so dirty it left a ring . . . after this I gotta condition it. I'mma put these eggs and hot oil and this conditioner through ya hair then wrap it up with this Saran Wrap so then you can raise up.

BERTA: How long that gone stay on my hair?

MOMMA: For about thirty minutes and then I gotta wash it out.

EXTRA 2: One hour and a half later Berta sits under the dryer.

BERTA: Momma, can I get out from under this dryer? My head burnin up.

MOMMA: Lemme see (*Runs her hand through* BERTA's *head*) Girl yo hair ain't dry yet. You got about thirty mo minutes.

EXTRA 3: Fofty-five minutes later Berta sits with a towel around her neck.

EXTRA 1: Two hot combs are on an electric stove. Her mother goes from one to the other, hot combing her hair to straighten it. The room is filled with smoke and they have both come to the end.

MOMMA: Berta when I say hold ya head down that means to look down. The only reason I'm doin it in the first place is cause ya daddy said he was taking you to the hair show and I don't want nobody comin to me talkin bout how come she ain't ready for her daddy? Or, the reason I didn't get to go with daddy is cause momma didn't have me ready. Nooo, you gone be ready and he don't like no nappy headed girls so-u-will-get-this-head-fixed-to-nite-or-my name ain't Angel Morning and-that-is-my-damn-name if he don't show up he ain't got nothin but his damn self to find fault with.

MOMMA *is pullin and yankin on* BERTA's *head. It seems as if it will fly off. It is electric. Thunder roars and* THE EXTRAS *walk on stage in full rain gear. They dance around* BERTA *and her mother. While the thunder and lightening increases, they pull out huge shears and begin snipping around* BERTA. *As soon as they begin snipping,* MOMMA *stops her rant and begins clawing at the falling hair.*

MOMMA: Berta! Berta! Berta! What have u done! Berta! BERTA!!!!! Nooooooo!

ANNOUNCER: And the winner of this year's Little Miss All That Hair On Yo Head issssssss . . . Little Miss Ebony Ginger Johnson. Her mother called this style teasin but pleasin . . . she's representing The Q-nee Homes Projects and sponsored by Clay and Jackson Funeral Homes . . . Taking care of yo loved ones eternally.

Loud cheers, flashing lights and applause.

Lights up MOMMA *sits with her back to the audience.* ADULT BERTA *walks on stage . . . with a shaved head.*

BERTA: Momma. It's been 12 years now. Don't you think this silence thing has gone a bit far? I said I was sorry. Look, momma, I'm about to graduate from college. That's something to be proud of. (*Beat*) I never believed in that—a woman's hair is her glory mumbo-jumbo. And I didn't wantta be in no dumb hair show . . . momma. OK, momma. Whenever you decide to talk again or sing . . . I miss your singing . . .

END OF PLAY

TISH BENSON ON HAIRSTORY

I knew this had to be off and running in thirty seconds . . . no fat. So for me, it was a pleasure to nail down something in my life that wasn't girth-heavy. But I was happy to share my work—especially in this format—because I hoped I would learn something . . .

The reason I wrote a memory piece about a daughter-mother relationship with doing hair as the main conflict was basic—it came to me to write. And my writing process just depends on what is being written—I have no rules, and that's a problem. But I'm interested in memories and how they shape who we are, and my style is countrified. I am interested in quirky characters who are honest even if they do dishonest things. And I prefer to be taken someplace I've never been before so that I'm not bored and loaded down with an idea that can't get out of its own way to tell the story.

READER QUESTIONS

1. There is a much different style, or "shape," as Dixon suggested, of storytelling in this play than in the others. What makes it different? And how does that difference enhance the theatricality of the play?

2. There's a chorus of Extras in *Hairstory*. What's their function? How do they serve the storytelling of the play?

3. The conflict of this play is woven in and out of the memories of Berta's past. At first glance, there might not seem to be a hard-edged story

conflict. Yet, we know there's dramatic tension that builds throughout the play. How does the playwright keep you engaged with the story and sustain the dramatic tension and internal conflict that resolves at the end?

4. Language seems to be a very important feature of this play, particularly as it relates to character. But aside from indicating the cultural or ethnic background of the characters, how else is language manipulated to indicate Berta's journey?

8

CHAPTER

Let's Get Jiggy with It

I prefer to be taken someplace I've never been before so that I'm not bored and loaded down with an idea that can't get out of its own way to tell the story.

—Tish Benson, playwright

OKAY. ENOUGH. I'VE TALKED ABOUT THEM, OTHER PEOPLE HAVE talked about them, and you've read five. You're probably up to your ears in information and stimulation. But I hope you're filled with inspiration as well. Now it's time to do it yourself. I want you to write a no-holds-barred, off the top of your head, first draft of a ten-minute play. And while I can't be watching over your shoulder, I'll hound you from these white pages. A word of caution: If you're not into this, don't do it. It'll be a waste of your time because you'll write something that you don't really care about and no matter how good of a writer you are, that will show. That's right: when you don't care about what you're writing, it's as obvious as a third eye in the middle of your forehead. But if you do want to give it a shot, let's get jiggy with it.

Before we take the smallest step forward, the first thing I want you to do is something most of us have the hardest time doing at the beginning of our work: think. So often we just want to jump to "start," a kind of not-looking-before-we're-leaping thing, wherein with wild abandonment we let our fingers fly across the keyboard and allow the story to magically appear. I promise you we'll get to that, but first I just want you to sit quietly and think for a moment about this: What's something you care about? I mean, *really* care about? Is there something that makes you angry, sad, or joyous at the very thought of it? Tired of how the world doesn't seem to give a shit about its youth and what's happening to their dot-com brains? Are you frightened by how fragile life is, and by the idea that in the tiniest instance, it can all be sniffed out? Do you look at your grandmother with adoring eyes and long to know all that she knows? Do you look at your boyfriend and wonder what your life would have been like if you hadn't spilled your coffee all over a then-stranger in your local diner? Are there questions about life burning in you somewhere to be answered? Is there some idea, some mystery you've always wanted to explore?

You have to write from a place in your heart where you can touch something that you really care about. Yeah, I know, you want to write a rip-roaring comedy; still, underneath it all, there has to be something that you want to say: divorce sucks, love hurts, Europe's overrated 'cause the ol' US of A is where it happens if it's worth happening. I say to my students: Jell-O in is Jell-O out. If you don't really care about what you're writing, neither will I. Think back on the five playwrights whose work you read in this book; reread their own thoughts about how they began writing what they wrote. They all wrote from a place of trying to understand something that was a question, curiosity, or passion for them. So if you've thought of your own question, curiosity, or passion that gets your juices flowing, let's get started. If you haven't, go to the gym and lift a couple of hundred pounds over your head. At least that'll be somewhat productive.

This is going to feel a little disjointed at first, but stick with it—it'll all blend together at the end. Okay, we're going to count this down like the takeoff it is:

Ten
Grab a pad of paper, or use your computer—whatever. Write in big letters the focus of your question/curiosity/passion, like: "WHAT DOES SUCCESS MEAN TO ME?" or "I LOVE THE UNEXPECTED," or "I'M LOOKING FOR LOVE IN ALL THE WRONG PLACES." Keep this in the back of your mind the whole time you're writing; maybe it'll show up somewhere, maybe it won't. But if you focus on it, it'll be there, rumbling underneath all you say and do.

Nine

Make up a person with an identity. Do it quick. Don't think much about it yet. Say something to yourself like, "I want to write an artist—a painter." Now make something up that the artist/painter really *wants*, really *needs* in his big life story: success, recognition, money. Now give him a real *reason* that he needs what he needs: he's been painting for twelve years and has gotten nowhere and he's losing his confidence. He can't even think of what he'd do if he weren't a painter.

Now stop; that's all you need to do for the moment on the artist. Yeah, I know. It feels all superficial and contrived at this point, but you'll layer it soon enough.

Next: think of two, three, or four other characters in the same exact quick way you thought of the artist. Like your central character, they all should want or need something in their lives in a significant way. Make it up if you have to. Don't try to make sense of it now. Just let something fly out of your imagination and on to the page. You can change it later if it doesn't fit the story of your play.

Eight

It can be drudgery, I know, but spend just an hour fleshing out all of your characters with microbiographies. I promise you, it won't be wasted time. Think about where they grew up, what their family life was like, where and how they were educated, or *if* they were formally educated. What religion do they believe in, if at all? What are their politics? What are their passions? Have they ever been in love? How many times? What are their weird, eccentric, secret quirks they don't want anyone to find out? Most importantly, what do they want or need right now, and why do they need it? Write all of this down. Don't try to make it sound pretty or resemble something you'd hand in to your English professor. Just let the thoughts flow. But do write it down; it's more concrete then.

Seven

Finesse the characters. Now, bend and shape what you've thought of in such a way that you can see the two, three or four characters in the same space at the same time with your central character—and make sure it seems logical. What would allow that? What circumstance could bring them together? What twist of fate, chance meeting, or innocent collision of their worlds will best focus back on the central character and whether that person will get what he or she wants in this story? If I'm using the example from step 9 of my painter who really wants and needs recognition, maybe I give him a wife who needs more of his attention (because she needs to feel loved), an agent who needs to get out of the art business and pursue his dream of flying (because he needs to be free of responsibility), and a best friend who thinks he needs to join the Hair Club for Men (because he needs to feel attractive). Can you see the conflict beginning to build itself? And you haven't really even started writing yet.

Six

A setting. Think of an *interesting, unusual* setting for your play. Take your lead from your central character. If I use the artist/painter example, I can always set the play in his studio or an art gallery. But what if I stick him in a waiting line at the Internal Revenue Service, or at a service counter for lawn mowers at Sears? What do I get when I take him out of the expected, and put him in an unexpected place we don't usually associate him with? And wherever you set your play, is it someplace where you can introduce your other characters with ease? Bend and shape it to make it so. Using my painter, if he's in a waiting line for the IRS, called in for who knows why, maybe his wife and best friend are with him. And maybe, just maybe, his agent shows up because he's being audited somewhere in the same building.

Five

Reassess everything. You've got a central character that wants/really needs something, and for the purpose of the ten-minute play, will either get it, not get it, or think of plan B by the play's end. You've got at least one other character in the play that needs and wants something too, and if you've thought it through, can somehow be responsible for helping the central character or hindering him from getting what he wants. You've created an interesting setting for everyone's world to collide in, and if you've been able to just let your mind wander, you've seen the smallest kernel of conflict beginning to form.

Four

Solidify the story as much as you can and be specific. Let your mind imagine all the possible directions the story could take. Toss around a lot of ideas. Play each idea out to find out what best makes sense for the characters you've created. When you settle on a semi-solid idea, make sure you're clear about it—or as clear as you can be at this point—by writing down the simple version of the story line. It might read something like this: "This is the story of a painter who desperately needs recognition from the art world but realizes in the course of the play that what he really needs is to be recognized—seen for what he is—by those who love him." It could also read something like this: "This is the story of a painter who, while being investigated for tax fraud by the IRS, discovers that his wife is having an affair with his best friend or his agent or, what he fears most, both." And of course, there's every variation in between and beyond these two examples. To be able to condense your story down to a simple one- or two-line description is a great exercise that forces you to get really clear about what you're writing.

Now take out your paper that we started this whole process with, the one that identifies your question/curiosity/passion. Think about it one more time, because it's time to start writing.

Three

Let's go for it. Don't get bogged down with a title; let the play inspire you later. Just start writing. Maybe you don't even know what you're going to write. That's okay. Just start writing.

Remember, the play has to have some sort of structure to it and since time is of the essence, try to start in the middle, not at the beginning. Or start at the end, and write backward to the beginning. Do whatever you want to do, but keep the structure thing in the front part of your brain and don't forget that you've got to have some sort of *driving action* (the central character growing more and more desperate to get what he wants) in the story that is complicated by other people, events beyond everyone's control, or life circumstances. And as you write along, *complicate* the story. Make it seem like the obstacles that keep the central character from getting what she wants are almost insurmountable.

Here's the coach in me: Now take us on a ride! Let us think we're going in one direction and surprise the hell out of us when you shift to another! Write the unexpected! Surprise us! Don't let me predict what's going to happen—that's boring. *Boring!* Keep us guessing what's going to happen next. Go, go, go! Don't be afraid to write too much. You can cut it back later. *Stop thinking!* Just write. Write until you have to stop. So what if you've only written three pages? Who cares? You'll write three more pages tomorrow. Do what you can, then pat yourself on the back.

Two

Finish the play. As muddy, confused, stupid, uninteresting, lame, and vile as you think it is, just finish the play. Don't go over what you've already written, just finish the play. Force yourself; it's the only way for you to know what you have and don't have to play with when you get down to the real skill of writing: rewriting.

One

You've got the first draft of a play. Congratulations. Yeah, I know you think it sucks. But now you have a chance to make it better. Answer all of these questions before beginning your rewrite:

1. Did I make it clear in the story that the central character wants something? Is the conflict clear?
2. Did I create enough obstacles that get in the way of the central character getting what she or he wants?
3. Is there a structure to the story that pushes the dramatic action forward, causing one event to lead to the next?
4. Is there any way that I can deepen or layer the characters? Can I give them behaviors that will make them both interesting and engaging to an audience? Is there something from their biographies that I can bring into the story that will add texture?
5. Is there something theatrical about the story? Am I using all the dramatic possibilities a stage, live actors, lighting, sound, scenery, and costumes can afford?
6. Do the characters sound different or do they all sound the same? Can I better use language to indicate their personalities?
7. Is there anything that I'm being stubborn about that doesn't belong in the story, but that I like anyway and should cut now before I become too attached to it?
8. Do I address in the play what I was passionate about before I started writing, no matter how subtle?

Blast Off

What can you say now? You can say you've written a ten-minute play, *if* you've edited your work down to ten pages. Is it good? Is it interesting? Is it engaging? Well, you probably won't know that for a while until you've reshaped the play five times over, brought more and more of your voice into its making, and then seen it read with actors, and if you're lucky, an audience. But at least you began something and are no longer carrying around an idea that you've had in your head for the last three years. Now go do something nice for yourself. We should always celebrate what seems like even our smallest victories. Blast off, baby.

9
CHAPTER

Ten Last Thoughts

If you're a writer, that's what you do. You can't bake a pan of lasagna and call it a play.

—Me, from *The Playwright's Survival Guide*

No fanfare; here they are:

1. There is something so unique and precious about you—you as a person, writer, friend, and companion. Don't lose that in your writing. It's what makes you special and different. Don't try to be someone else's idea of a writer. Be yourself. That's what I want to see in your writing.

2. You're the only person that can write your play with the vision that you have of the story. Listen to what others have to say; take in their advice. But don't write anyone's version of your play but yours. A play written by committee is hardly a play at all.

3. Learn the difference between when your ego is listening to criticism and when your writer's heart and soul are. If you're unsure of yourself, ask a friend you trust to tell you when your ego's getting in the way.

4. Write from the heart, then from the head. You can't go wrong. I'll always marvel and admire you for your insight into the human condition, but I can only applaud you for turning a witty phrase.

5. When in doubt, read. Read as many plays, books about playwrights, and books about the theatre as you can find. Learn from the people

who've been there, are there, and are looking to stay there. They've got something important to share.

And on the ten-minute play:

6. Ten minutes is ten pages, *maximum*. Cheating gets you nowhere you want to be.

7. Remember, somebody has to eventually produce what you've written, so be sensible.

8. A ten-minute play has all the good dramatic elements that a longer play has.

9. Care about what you're writing about; it shows up even in a ten-minute play.

10. Once you've mastered this form, go on to the next. We need writers in the theatre that can write longer plays.

CONCLUSION, WITH HISTORY

HERE'S ME CONCLUDING BY TAKING YOU IN FOR A HISTORY LESSON. Here's you kicking and screaming and making blubbery noises. Buck up; this won't take long, and y'might even learn something.

Take heed, you MTV finger pointers: lest we be so shortsighted as to think that the collapsing of the dramatic form is our own invention, we have to look no further back than turn-of-the-nineteenth-century Broadway. In the early 1800s, Appia and Craig were redefining the concepts of stage design; Antoine's *Theatre Libre* introduced the world to the independent theatre model; and the commercialization of the world's larger theatres was in full swing. The theatre world was exploding with ideas but had fewer venues than ever to explore them.

Enter the Little Theatre Movement.

Writing in 1917, Constance D'arcy Mackay had this to say about the Little Theatre Movement:

> The newest and most vital note in the art of the United States today is struck by that arch-foe of commercialism—the Little Theater . . . [The Little Theater movement is] the newest, freest, most potent and democratic force in the art of the American stage. (Mackay iii, 1)

Yeah, yeah, yeah . . . but who cares about a crunchy old theatre movement? And what were they doing in the first place? In fact, they were doing three things, all of which will sound oh-so-familiar to today's theatre artisans:

1: Responding to Broadway Commercialism

In 1917, Sheldon Cheney wrote:

> Whereas Broadway is concerned with a journalistic product—direct, obviously appealing, sensational, ephemeral . . . the art theatres are . . . devoted primarily to something subtler and more specialized in its appeal . . . It is the most hopeful thing in the theatre world today, because its roots are in native soil and because it is reaching up beyond those realms of commerce and materialism in which the business theatre constantly exists. (18, 124)

The Little Theatre Movement was local, relevant, accessible, and vital. Then, like now, theatre artists wanted to innovate. In their case, they wanted to oppose the star system and bring about a true ensemble—actors, designers, writers, and directors working collectively. The Little Theatre Movement brought together like-minded people quickly, creatively, and energetically and brought in like-minded audiences. By the 1920s, more than fifty independent American theatres produced shows for their own subscriber bases in such venues as the Chicago Little Theatre, the Boston Toy Theatre, the New York Little Theatre, New York's Neighborhood Playhouse, New York's Washington Square Players, and the Provincetown Playhouse.

2: Championing New and Emerging Voices

What, you thought ours was the first generation to see big theatres that wouldn't take risks on untried artists? You thought we were the first theatre folks to experience development/workshop/staged reading hell? Puhleez. Even in turn-of-the-century America, no one could afford a turkey; risk aversion was key to staying alive. Then, like now, festivals and neighborhood productions gave emerging artists a chance to showcase themselves. Perhaps the best example of this was the Provincetown Playhouse: less than a decade after its foundation, the Provincetown Players had staged ninety-three new plays by forty-seven writers.

3: Allowing for the Diversity of Works and Participants

The commercialization of Broadway marginalized theatre participants across the board. The Littler Theatre Movement sought to change that. For example, the Negro Players, a Little Theatre, gave African Americans in the United States their first opportunity to perform plays interpretive of their own race—no doubt a welcome change for black actors wanting greater depth and variation than the roles provided by the likes of *Showboat* and *Uncle Tom's Cabin*.

Innovation. New voices. Diversity. If these words don't describe the last ten-minute festival you sat through, I don't know what does.

What does the work of a bunch of dead theatre artists have to do with you? Plenty. In addition to bringing about off-Broadway experimentation, developing a relationship between artisans and audiences, and fore-grounding the works of American dramatists, the greatest legacy of America's Little Theatre Movement is its popularization of the one-act form. Not because it was innovative and wacky. Not because the seats were god-awful uncomfortable and no one could sit still for five-hour shows. And not because people had discovered radio and thereby lost their collective ability to think for themselves.

The artists of the Little Theatre Movement pushed the one-act form out front because they understood that the more varied the program, the more opportunities for people to show off their skills. In the course of a single evening, several one-acts could go up, thereby showcasing hundreds of artists. What's more, the cost—and risk—of producing an evening could be shared by lots of different groups. The end result? Audiences were exposed to loads of new artists, and artists got a shot at honing their respective crafts in a real way.

Enter present day.

As an emerging, untried theatre artist, what's your best shot at being produced? Is it your full-length musical ode to the universe? Probably not. Is it your operatic, all-Nazi aquacade, replete with cannon fire and extras on horseback? Doubt it. More than likely, your shot at entering the fray hails from the estimated one zillion workshops, readings, and festivals that embrace the short form. Do you have more than ten minutes' worth of something to say? Probably. Will you get to say it one day? Hopefully. What's your best route to get there? Pick a ten-minute festival. Any ten-minute festival.

So, the next time someone's playing the point-and-click-mentality, video-killed-the-radio-star blame game, just remember that the short-ened dramatic form emerged from a real need—to not adhere to Broadway ideals, to give lots of folks a chance to be heard and hone their crafts, and to open up the theatre to all communities who wanted to find themselves there. However brief the form, and however short-lived the genre, there's always some method to the madness.

CITATIONS

Cheney, Sheldon. *The Art Theatre*. New York: Alfred A. Knopf, 1917.

Mackay, Constance D'arcy. *The Little Theatre in the United States*. New York: Henry Holt and Company, 1917.

BIOGRAPHIES

TISH BENSON, poet and playwright, graduated from New York University's Dramatic Writing Program in 1999 with an MFA in playwriting. Her forthcoming book of poetry and short stories, *Lil' This Lil' That Some of the Other*, is being published by Big Drum Press. Other plays include *Boxed*, *Thila Nicee and Ralph*, *Watch and Snippets of Scenicville, Texas*. Her play *Hairstory* is being made into a short film by Montage Productions.

For rights, contact the author in care of the Dramatic Writing Program, 721 Broadway, 7th Floor, New York, NY 10003.

DAVID CRESPY is an assistant professor of playwriting in the University of Missouri–Columbia Department of Theatre and serves as the artistic director of MU's Missouri Playwrights Workshop. His play *Perfect Hair* was recently read as part of the 10-Minute Play Fringe Festival at the 2000 Last Frontier Theatre Conference in Valdez, Alaska, under the direction of Michael Warren Powell. His play *Beshert* won a Panelist's Choice award at the same conference. David was a cofounder and former artistic director of the WaterFront Ensemble, Inc., a professional nonprofit organization dedicated to the development of new plays located in Hoboken, New Jersey. His play *Men Dancing* received the 1996 21st Century Playwrights Award. David is a recipient of an MU Summer Research Fellowship for his play *Tekiyá*. Other plays include *The Source of All Our Goodness*, *Meadow*, *Shot Dead*, *Stampede*, *Hierarchy of Angels*, *The Queen's Orphans*, *In Transit* (*The Coast Line*, *Long Rider*, *Cross the Hudson*), *Jersey Shore*, *The Zenith Escape*, *Lantuchs & Laughter*, *Seven Were Hanged*, and *Penny Dreadful*.

Agent contact: Robert Duva, Duva-Flack Associates, 200 W. 57th St., Suite 1008, New York, NY 10019. (212) 957-9600

GARY SUNSHINE's plays include A *History of Plastic Slipcovers*, *Bigger Than You*, and *Mercury*. His work has been seen at New York Theatre Workshop's Just Add Water Festival, the Flea, the Directors Company, Spectrum Stage, and the Cherry Lane Alternative. With Eve Ensler, Gary coedited and arranged *Borrowed Light*, a performance piece of works written by a group of women inmates at the Bedford Hills Correctional Facility. AB: Princeton. MFA: Dramatic Writing Program at NYU's Tisch School of the Arts (Harry Kondoleon Graduate Playwriting Prize, New York Picture Company Award for Best Dramatic Screenplay).

For rights, contact the author in care of the Dramatic Writing Program, 721 Broadway, 7th Floor, New York, NY 10003.

MICHEL WALLERSTEIN was born and raised in Lausanne, Switzerland, where he attended his first year of law school before coming to New York. He graduated from NYU Film School in 1982 and has remained in New York ever since. Michel writes primarily for European film and television (MOWs and drama series). His latest movie of the week, *Last Wish*, written with partner Linda Wendell for RTL Television, has been selected for the Munich TV Film Festival. He discovered the joy of writing for theatre relatively recently, when he completed his first full-length play, *Five Women Waiting* (produced by the Open Door Theatre). His first ten-minute play, *Lapdance*, was produced at Pulse Ensemble Theatre (NYC), Expanded Arts (NYC), and the Turnip Festival (NYC). His one-act, *Boomerang*, was produced at Expanded Arts (NYC). Michel is looking forward to producing all five ten-minute plays due to appear in Gary Garrison's *Perfect 10: Writing and Producing the Ten-Minute Play* in early 2001 along with Garrison's short play *Cherry Reds*.

WENDY YONDORF is a recipient of the Berilla Kerr Foundation Award for her playwriting. Her first full-length play, *The Space Between the Trees*, produced by Niagara University, was nominated by the Kennedy Center's American College Theatre Festival as a regional finalist. Her one-acts, *The Twin* and 8 *Across* were most recently produced by Circle Lab and Westside

Arts Theatres in New York City. Her full-length 13 RITES was part of the Festival of New Play/New Voices at La Mama, Etc., and a scene from the play was published by Heinemann in *Scenes for Women by Women*. Her new play, *Lupus Quadrille*, will be read at the 78th Street Theatre Lab. Wendy came to playwriting after fifteen years of acting in film, television, and on stage, and doing stand-up comedy and voice-overs. She is a member of Circle Repertory Lab, Lanford Wilson's Playwright's Retreat, 78th Street Theatre Group–Foreplay, the Dramatist's Guild, SAG, and AEA. Wendy has just completed a screenplay, *Signature of a Where*.

Agent contact: Ron Gwiazda, Rosenstone/Wender, 3 East 48th Street, New York, NY 10017. (212) 832-8330

Any questions or comments about *Perfect 10: Writing and Producing the Ten-Minute Play*? Contact the author at his website <www.garygarrison.com>.